Praise for *Saying No and Letting Go: Jewish Wisdom on Making Room for What Matters Most* by Rabbi Edwin Goldberg, DHL

"If you wish you had more t̲ ̲ ̲ ̲ ̲ ̲ ̲ ̲ ̲ ̲ ̲ ̲ ̲ ̲ *any* time—to stop and think about what you really want your life to be, please read this wise, insightful and often funny book. It won't take you long. It *will* help you figure out what truly matters to you and—more important—what doesn't."
—**Dave Barry**, Pulitzer Prize-winning author, columnist and humorist

"In the midst of our increasingly harried technological world, Rabbi Goldberg provides a moving and inspiring meditation on how to stay focused on what's actually important."
—**Rabbi Jill Jacobs**, executive director, Truah: The Rabbinic Call for Human Rights; author, *Where Justice Dwells: A Hands-On Guide to Doing Social Justice in Your Jewish Community*

"Rabbi Goldberg makes it crystal clear that 'making room for what matters most' requires abundant wisdom and insight, but also equal amounts of willingness and humor. His own wisdom and insights reflected in excellent choices of sacred and secular stories and vivid examples prepare us to struggle less and live more. I highly recommend [this] book for anyone ready to do more with less."
—**Rabbi David Lyon**, senior rabbi, Congregation Beth Israel, Houston, Texas; author, *God of Me: Imagining God throughout Your Lifetime*

"A lovely book! Skillfully weaves Jewish concepts, contemporary stories and heartfelt insights into a highly readable charge to reduce the burdens in our lives in order to realize our full potential as human beings. A must read for those seeking a path to unclutter the heart and liberate the mind."
—**Dr. Ron Wolfson**, Fingerhut Professor of Education, American Jewish University; author, *Relational Judaism: Using the Power of Relationships to Transform the Jewish Community*

"When we let go of distractions that make us busy, activities that make us inattentive and resentments that cause us pain, we create space within our psyches and souls for a life with more meaning.... [This] book teaches us that when we let go of things, thoughts and time wasted, we make room for a life of beauty and goodness."
—**Rabbi Karyn D. Kedar**, author, *God Whispers: Stories of the Soul, Lessons of the Heart* and *The Bridge to Forgiveness: Stories and Prayers for Finding God and Restoring Wholeness*

"Provides a thoughtful, well-reasoned and Jewishly grounded approach on how to remain true to one's deepest values while easing the overwhelming and ever-present pressures of everyday life. It's a practical guide to help you to be genuinely yourself while navigating the emotional challenges of twenty-first-century living. *Nesia Tova!*"
—**Dr. Misha Galperin**, CEO and president, Jewish Agency International Development; author, *Reimagining Leadership in Jewish Organizations: Ten Practical Lessons to Help You Implement Change and Achieve Your Goals*

"In our American culture, 'no' is felt to be a denial of freedom and an assault on our autonomy. Rabbi Edwin Goldberg, drawing on Jewish teachings and tradition, suggests that 'saying no' frees up space, opens potential and liberates time so that we can grow into the people we truly want to be, and ought to be. Self-limitation is an invitation to expansive possibility, ease of spirit and joy. This is a practice we can all use—today."
—**Rabbi Jonathan P. Slater**, co-director of programs, Institute for Jewish Spirituality

"Is your life frenetic and full?... Do your kids go to bed before you get home from work? Do you chat regularly on Facebook but seldom have time to meet friends for coffee? If you answered yes to any of these questions then this book is for you. Rabbi Goldberg introduces us to centuries of time-tested Jewish wisdom in order to help us rediscover our personal missions and realign our lives with our core values. PS: If you don't have time to read this book, know that he wrote it for you."
—**Rabbi Jamie Korngold**, author, *The God Upgrade: Finding Your 21st-Century Spirituality in Judaism's 5,000-Year-Old Tradition*

Saying No
and No
Letting Go

Jewish Wisdom
on
Making Room
for **What**
Matters Most

RABBI EDWIN GOLDBERG, DHL

FOREWORD BY RABBI NAOMI LEVY

Author of *To Begin Again* and *Talking to God*

For People of All Faiths, All Backgrounds

JEWISH LIGHTS Publishing

Woodstock, Vermont

Saying No and Letting Go:
Jewish Wisdom on Making Room for What Matters Most

2013 Quality Paperback Original, First Printing
© 2013 by Edwin Goldberg
Foreword © 2013 by Naomi Levy

Library of Congress Cataloging-in-Publication Data

Goldberg, Edwin C.
  Saying no and letting go : Jewish wisdom on making room for what matters most / Rabbi Edwin Goldberg, DHL; foreword by Rabbi Naomi Levy.
      pages cm
  Includes bibliographical references.
  ISBN 978-1-58023-670-6
  1. Jewish way of life. 2. Spiritual life—Judaism. I. Title.
  BM723.G6135 2013
  296.7—dc23
                                    2012050270

10 9 8 7 6 5 4 3 2 1

Manufactured in the United States of America

Cover Design: Heather Pelham

Published by Jewish Lights Publishing
A Division of LongHill Partners, Inc.
Sunset Farm Offices, Route 4, P.O. Box 237
Woodstock, VT 05091
Tel: (802) 457-4000   Fax: (802) 457-4004
www.jewishlights.com

Elegance is refusal.

—DIANA VREELAND

I awake each day torn between a desire to save the world
or savor the world. It makes it hard to plan the day.

—E. B. WHITE

Contents

Foreword

We all want to live a full life, but what are we to do when life becomes too full? We are overworked and overextended, and our thoughts are scattered. Technology is blurring the lines between work and home, and peace seems like a far-off dream.

How do we regain our focus? How do we reclaim balance? How do we make room for rest? The book in your hands, *Saying No and Letting Go,* offers us a path to sanity and a return to love and meaningful relationships. In the pages that follow you will learn ways to restore your focus and recapture your true authentic vision. You will learn the power of Shabbat and the meaning of holiness.

When chaos threatens to overwhelm us, we have a choice. Rabbi Edwin Goldberg offers us the ancient mystical art of *tzimtzum,* or contraction. We learn that gathering ourselves up can transform us from a diluted self to a state of concentration and focus and truth. Through contraction we make room—for others, for God, for miracles, and for surprise. By contracting we actually grow. We learn to hear what others are really trying to say to us, we learn to hear the voice of our own souls, and we learn to hear the voice of God calling out to us.

The word "no" can be quite difficult to utter, but it is the key to a life of boundaries. We must learn how to use it with others, but also how to say it to ourselves. Wanting more can lead us down a path to misery and envy. How else is it possible that we can have so much and still feel so empty?

Set limits, pull back, set aside time for rest, move from chaos to focus, say no, listen to what you've been ignoring, make room for what you've been longing for and you will uncover the true meaning of the word "full." A whole life is waiting for you.

Set aside the time to read this book in peace and quiet. Within it you will find a path back to your own life.

—Rabbi Naomi Levy

Introduction

I recently discovered a restaurant that serves only beer, and a tantalizing variety of beer, too. What makes this establishment different from other beer joints is that it sells absolutely *no* food. If you're hungry, however, you need not despair. Every so often waiters or waitresses from a number of nearby restaurants will walk up to your table and ask if you would like to order something from their menu. If you're interested, they will take your order and your money (or credit card) and in a short while return with your food.

Let's think about this for a moment. The owners of the beer joint realized that they were really good at selling beer. That's what they do. So instead of selling wonderful beer and second-rate food, they decided to collaborate with other businesses and literally allow employees from these places to cross their threshold, serve their customers, and take money that normally would go to the bar.

In order for this business model to succeed, the beer folks have to give up some control of the experience their customers have in their establishment. I like to imagine that back in the planning stages, they had an "aha" moment when they realized that by letting go of what is usually a crucial part of a restaurant's mission, they could focus on what mattered most to them.

The irony here is that the name of the restaurant is World of Beer. In the traditional mystical conception of God creating the world, taught by Rabbi Isaac Luria in the sixteenth century, God decides that the only way the world can exist is for God to relinquish control over the world. In Hebrew, this willful letting go of control is called *tzimtzum*.

Divine Contraction and What It Means for Us

What is *tzimtzum*? To make a complicated thing as simple as possible, imagine that God created the universe and that God was absolutely everywhere. There was no inch that was not filled with the Divine Spirit. How could anything else exist? In order to create space for the rest of creation (including you and me), God voluntarily withdrew from much of the universe, leaving room for us.

Students of Rabbi Isaac Luria, the sixteenth-century sage who devised this theory, have debated whether this imagery should be taken literally or metaphorically, but for our purposes it is the metaphor that suffices. In order for good things to happen (e.g., creation), space must be made.

Ever find yourself in a conversation where you cannot get a word in edgewise? That's really frustrating, isn't it? Or attend a party where one person clearly dominates the room? How quickly does that get tiresome? They used to say of Theodore Roosevelt that he had to be the bride at every wedding and the corpse at every funeral. Such solipsism is exhausting. However, when we willingly contract our personality in order to allow others to communicate and even shine, the energy in the room seems to grow. This is what I would call a modern example of *tzimtzum*. It is said that a young woman found herself having dinner one week in nineteenth-century England with William Gladstone one night and Benjamin Disraeli another night. Since both men were vying for the post of prime minister, a reporter asked the woman to compare the two men. She replied that dining with Gladstone made her feel that he was the most important person in the world. Dining with Disraeli, on the other hand, made her feel that *she* was the most important person in the world. Guess who won the election? Guess who practiced a form of *tzimtzum*?

I once had a teacher at the Hebrew University of Jerusalem who said that every good teacher needs to learn how to cheat. By this he did not mean inflating grades or some other questionable practice, but rather that teachers have to hold back in order to give only part of what they know. After all, the idea is for the student to learn, not for the teacher to pour out everything he or she knows. The complex details of the philosophical/mystical teachings of Isaac Luria are beyond the scope of this book, so please allow me to "cheat" and share with you only one aspect of *tzimtzum* as it appears in one Jewish text. The specific source is the great Hasidic rabbi Nachman of Breslov (c. 1772). A great-grandson of the Baal Shem Tov, the founder of Hasidic Judaism, Nachman of Breslov placed great emphasis on living with faith and joy. Rejecting hereditary authority, he left no physical heirs, but his teachings still garner great respect. He wrote:

> Now when God decided to create [the world], there was no place in which to create a world; everything, everywhere, there was but Endless God. So He withdrew His light to the sides in the process of *tzimtzum,* thus creating an empty space. Within the empty space He brought forth all the "days" and "measures," beginning the process of the world's creation. Now without this empty space there could be no world, as there would have been no room for creation at all.
>
> This *tzimtzum,* the empty space, cannot be easily understood by our human minds because two contradictory statements must be made concerning it: an "it is" and an "it is not." For the empty space comes about through *tzimtzum,* through God's withdrawing His self from there. There is, as it were, no God there. For if this were not so, there would be no *tzimtzum,* all would be endless God, and there would be no place for the creation of the world at all. But in the truth of truth, God must be there as well—for there is nothing at all without God's life in it. And that is why the empty space will not be understood until the future.[1]

There is something of a Zen koan about this teaching. A Zen koan is a paradoxical statement designed to move the initiate out of left-brain thinking. A classic example: "We know the sound of two hands clapping; but what is the sound of one hand clapping?" Reb Nachman's teaching reminds us that God is everywhere, and yet if God is everywhere, how can we be anywhere? The answer is that God removed God's self from creation so we can exist. And yet God is still everywhere. This contradiction cannot be resolved with logic, but for Nachman it is nonetheless true. The empty space is not devoid of God and yet must be empty for us to exist. In order to resolve this contradiction, we will have to wait for the messianic era.

In her book *The Murmuring Deep,* Israeli scholar Aviva Zornberg suggests that our understanding of reality is limited:

Beit Ya'akov (R. Ya'akov Leiner) ... amplifies the [following] concept: God accepts human ways of worship, which place individuality and free will at the center. But from a mystical point of view, this is an illusion, or a concept tailored to human thinking: there is only God and the divine energy that moves all things. And yet God chooses to be satisfied, seduced by the illusion of human consciousness and free will. He thus models for man a similar humility, accepting the restricted roles of conscious life.

The human being may be in the image of God, but paradoxically he comes to achieve that identity only by fragmentary and limited enactments. Even the omniscient God can come to know His own heart as well as the hearts of volatile human beings by improvising roles of restricted knowledge. [For example,] both analyst and analysand must relinquish a masterful knowledge if meaningful knowledge is to emerge. The analyst may understand the problem of his analysand from the beginning. But he finds a place of not-knowing, from which to work together with his analysand and in resistance to him, so that vital knowledge may be born.

... This is *tzimtzum* in a psychoanalytical sense: God withdraws from the presumption of total power and knowledge to leave a play area in which human worlds can be created. Gaps open up, absences, where God, apparently, is not.[2]

This is how I would render the message of the above texts: We really do not understand the reality before us. All we can hope to accomplish—by paying attention—is to learn to live with the mystery, become more comfortable with not knowing, and try to enjoy life's uncertainty. Every day is a gift, but we often squander it by missing what matters most. The goal of this book, through story and shared reflection, is to help you practice the discipline of letting go so you can enjoy real life. I say *enjoy,* even though real life is often unpleasant. But isn't there a kind of joy in being present? Isn't there a victory in dealing with what is really happening? True life necessarily involves denial of the many so we can enjoy the precious few. This is, in part, the teaching of the mystics. It can be our wisdom, too.

For us, *tzimtzum* means not responding to everything that comes our way. It means keeping silent more often. It means forgiving more. It means remembering that old saw: In life, takeaway *is* the takeaway. Ultimately, it means being like God: Just as God must withdraw to create room for us, so we withdraw to create room for others and for our most genuine selves.

In a world of seemingly scarce resources, *tzimtzum*—making room for what is most important in life—is wise, efficient, and foolproof. And the best part? We can start right now.

Pulling Back, Taking Control

I once heard it said that human beings spend the first three years of their lives thinking that they are the center of the universe, that they can have everything they want, and then they spend the rest of their lives trying to cope with the fact that they cannot (which might explain why adolescents seem angry so much of the time). Growing in wisdom allows us to lament the gap between wanting it all and having to make choices, but also to mature into a state of far lower expectations. The notion of *tzimtzum* is especially helpful in this regard because we are placed in the seat of control. We get to make the choice to contract, to limit what we do, based on what matters most. We all have limited resources, especially when it comes to time (the same 168 hours a week for everyone); therefore, there may be nothing more important than figuring out what are our top priorities and releasing our hold on everything else.

To clarify this concept, consider these examples of *tzimtzum* in real-life situations.

> **Item:** *Knifing the baby* is an extremely graphic term, employed by Silicon Valley technology companies, to describe the difficult task of killing a beloved project despite its popularity. One famous example is when Steve Jobs, newly returned to Apple Computer, declared that the company would no longer continue developing a PDA device to compete against the Palm Pilot. Jobs argued that the energy spent on this endeavor was taking away from the efforts to create an exciting new MP3 player. So, despite fervent protests from much of his staff, the PDA was shelved, and soon after the iPod was born. Not a bad bargain in the end.

> **Item:** *George Washington is a coward.* Despite his blatantly obvious bravery in the French and Indian War and in the War for Independence, many of Washington's fellow Americans could not understand why he refused to attack the British troops that would taunt him. Washington countered that he was following the example of the ancient Roman general who refused to engage in a battle he could not win. The general understood that America's ragtag army could never survive if he did not pass up many potential victories and wait for a sure thing.

> **Item:** *Only disconnect.* I recently spent five days on a silent retreat. The silent part was not too hard for me, but the idea

of not checking e-mails or enjoying my iPad struck terror in my heart. In the end, I realized that I needed to create more opportunities to be unplugged. Saying no to the temptations of modern technology is very hard, and many of us are ensnared by the seduction of always being connected to the outside world. But at what price?

The purpose of this book is to help you engage in a process of *tzimtzum*, willfully pulling back in order to regain control of the things that matter most. The formula for such work is simple: Find the space in your life to discover what your core values are and, through that discovery, what you want in your life. Second, identify the things you therefore cannot pursue, the opportunities you must willfully deny for the greater good. Third, practice the discipline of adhering to your choice. (*No* really means no.)

A Lesson from Mt. Everest

At 29,028 feet high, Mt. Everest's weather is seldom ideal for long, but the longest windows for ascent normally occur in the spring, from late March to the first week in June. This means that all those who want to climb the highest real estate on Earth need to make their attempts within that time frame. The extended time near the summit also increases the likelihood that people will succumb to other maladies related to high altitude, such as cerebral edema.

When climbers are near the peak, some persist in their summit attempt despite the threat of dangerous changes in weather conditions and the warnings of guides. Having spent tens of thousands of dollars on the expedition and so much energy getting up there, when conditions turn against them on the descent, they don't have enough energy to deal with getting down safely.

In his book, *Great by Choice,* Jim Collins recounts the story of the IMAX team that was filming a movie on Mt. Everest. In 1996, when many climbers died during a freak storm, no one in the IMAX crew was killed. Why not? Their leader had practiced the art of *tzimtzum*. At least that is what I would call it. He knew that making this movie was very important, but he also realized that keeping everyone safe was even more important. When he had to make a choice between risking the movie or his people, he relinquished the pursuit of the movie. At 2:00 p.m. (a previously determined time), he ordered everyone down from the final approach to the top. The weather was picture-perfect, and millions of dollars might be lost if the team did not push on to the summit. The team leader, however, knew that what mattered most was the lives of his crew, so he said no to any other desire. No really meant no. It could not have been an easy call.

Even without such a dramatic challenge before us (I would hope, anyway), all of us still make choices every day that entail saying no. *Tzimtzum* as a practice can help us ensure that we are aware of the choices we are making, and it can also help us find the discipline to keep saying no when it is the right thing to do.

In the chapters that follow, we will examine various ways that *tzimtzum* can apply to our lives. We will explore the weekly opportunity to embrace more holiness in life by intentionally pulling away from the world. We will understand how withdrawing from much of the world will make it possible for us to enjoy the most important gifts the world has to offer. We will see how downsizing our lifestyle, as well as jettisoning some of our emotional baggage, will free up more space for what is paramount in our lives. We will learn to respond to the important questions and not necessarily the choices put before us by others. We will even see how we can place our own limitations into a healthier perspective. We can learn to judge less, worry less, and fear less.

This collection of personal musings is informed to various degrees by Jewish wisdom gained from my life as a Reform Jew and a congregational rabbi, as well as drawn from the sacred texts of the Jewish tradition. It is loosely organized and doesn't require linear, start-to-finish reading. Dive into the chapter that speaks to you at the moment; revisit chapters that address topics you struggle with. While the content will resonate most strongly with Jews, its wisdom is accessible to people of all faiths who are looking for new perspectives on how to pare down their lives to what matters most.

Taming Our Focus

One more thought before we begin: Ever wonder why lion tamers take into the cage a chair as well as a whip and a gun? The whip makes sense (so does the gun). But why the chair? Remember that the chair is always held with the bottom of the four legs facing the lion. Because the lion tries to focus on all four points at the same time, he loses the ability to attack. In other words, because the lion cannot get focused, he cannot do what he might like to do. This is good news for the lion tamer but also instructive for us. We cannot accomplish our goals, we cannot become the people we are intended to become, if we cannot focus our lives. And the only way to do so is to learn to say no and let go.

1

Reconnect with the Holiness in Time

A young preacher was brand-new to his job. He was asked by the local funeral director to hold a graveside burial service at a small cemetery in the city. The deceased had no family or friends. The preacher left to go to the place early but quickly got lost, making several wrong turns.

Eventually arriving a half-hour late, he saw a backhoe and its crew, but the hearse was nowhere in sight, and the workers were eating lunch.

The diligent young pastor went to the open grave and found the vault lid already in place. Taking out his book, he read the service. Feeling guilty because of his tardiness, he preached an impassioned and lengthy eulogy, sending the deceased to the great beyond in grand style.

But as he was returning to his car, he overheard one of the workers say, "I've been putting in septic tanks for twenty years and I ain't never seen nothin' like that."

Lost in the (Spiritual) Wilderness

I am sure that even if such an event has never happened to us, we have all found ourselves doing the wrong thing at the wrong time in the wrong place. There is nothing new in that feeling. What may be new, however, is how often we get lost these days. I don't mean physically lost. Thanks to such devices as the GPS, we need never lose our geographic position, even if we would like to spend a little time "off the grid." I am referring to a spiritual wilderness, to a feeling that we cannot find our center, the concern that our days go by and we have less and less control over our lives.

I recently came across this list of the symptoms of these crazy days. See if any of these sound like you. You know you're living in this era because:

1. You accidentally enter your password on the microwave.

2. You haven't played solitaire with real cards in years.

3. You have a list of fifteen phone numbers to reach your family of three.

4. You e-mail or text the person who works at the desk next to you.

5. Your reason for not staying in touch with friends and family is that they don't have e-mail addresses or Facebook accounts.

6. You pull into your driveway and use your cell phone to see if anyone is home to help you carry in the groceries.

7. Leaving the house without your cell phone, which you didn't have the first twenty or thirty (or sixty) years of your life, is now a cause for panic and you turn around to go and get it.

8. You get up in the morning and go online before getting your coffee.[1]

What makes us live with such craziness? (And please know that I am as guilty of this anyone. Just ask my wife.) Why do we lose sight of who we are? What makes it okay to live with such a skewed perspective? Why do we allow ourselves to live our lives chained to machines?

I remember a few years ago when the BlackBerry system crashed throughout the country. To the delight of many frustrated spouses and children, BlackBerry owners were bereft of the source of their central preoccupation. It was a nightmare. But why? Why do these machines beguile us so? What is happening in our world that makes us such willing slaves to this technology?

Seduced by the Fruit of 24/7 Living

I don't have to look very far to find another major symptom of today's malaise. It's literally across the street from my home. My neighbors are building a McMansion on spec. Now, I expect the builders to work on Saturday, even if it is my Sabbath. I know we are not living in Israel. But when they show up on Sunday morning at 7:00 a.m. and start hammering away, I know that something in our society has gone seriously awry.

There was a time when it was almost considered a sacrilege to find a store open on Christmas Day, the Fourth of July, or Thanksgiving—not to mention Sundays. Today, it's not strange to hear terms like *24/7,* referring to stores open for business twenty-four hours a day. God only knows if stores can break even with such hours. How many people will visit a Walmart at 3:00 a.m. for holiday shopping?

Here's another concern: Despite the enormous market for cookware, cookbooks, and TV cooking programs, more people are eating out at fast-food restaurants (actually, taking home dinner from the drive-through windows) than at any other time.

"Hurry up! Hurry up! I can't lose any more time." That's the refrain of our era. The result? Nervous breakdowns and cardiac arrests; ulcers and chronic indigestion; chronic fatigue syndrome as well as divorces, teenage pregnancies, and the use of crack cocaine. Are these the fruits of our 24/7 lifestyle?

What madness has overtaken us? Remember that, in terms of technology, we are only at the beginning stages of our advancement. What will the future bring? *BusinessWeek,* in an issue devoted to the subject of work points out that in the coming years we will see Apple's iPhone shrunk down to the size of a credit card and connecting us to billions of pea-sized wireless sensors attached to buildings, streets, retail products, and our coworkers' and business partners' clothes—all sending data over the Net to us.[2]

It will be like that scene in Steven Spielberg's *Minority Report,* where no one can escape the steady drone of Madison Avenue appeals, plugged right into our retinas. As they say, "There's no cure for progress!"

For some, this will be a world of empowered individuals encased in a bubble of time-saving technologies. For most, it will be a world of virtual sweatshops, where we are always online and every keystroke, contact, and purchase is tracked. There will be no escape from the marketplace, the job, and even our social connections.

And this is something to look forward to? I don't think so. Contemplating our present, and this dire future, it seems as if we are as lost as that poor preacher eulogizing a septic tank!

In the unstoppable business of modern life, we have sacrificed that vital rhythm between work and rest. Our desire to succeed means we do not rest. Our culture, in which action equals accomplishment, demands the 24/7 lifestyle. And because we do not rest, we have lost our way. We have poisoned our lives because we believe that good things come only from tireless effort and continuous communication. We are seduced by the promises of more success, more money, more satisfaction, and more possessions.

There is a clear downside to all this technological frenzy. These machines are working us to death. Let's remember that the Chinese pictograph for *busy* is composed of two characters: heart and killing.

We should also remember the price we pay for our craziness. Consider the case of Susan Lawley, a woman who seemed to have it all. She was a vice president at the investment and securities firm Goldman Sachs. She supervised the administration of the firm's mortgage securities department, she had a six-figure income, she owned homes in New Jersey and on Long Island, and she vacationed with her husband and eleven-year-old son every year in Europe. One day, driving home in the rain, she cried so hard she could not see the road. She told a *New York Times* reporter, "I realized that tonight, like almost every night, I would miss seeing my son because he was already in bed. I realized that life is too short to live like that." A few weeks later she gave up her job and set up her own human resources consulting firm closer to home.[3]

Restoring the Rhythm of Work and Rest

Susan Lawley knew that she needed to restore balance in her life. She needed to determine what mattered most and practice *tzimtzum*. Instead of inventing something new, I would argue that we should begin by adapting some kind of Sabbath practice. In Judaism, the Sabbath—or Shabbat—is not only a day of the week. It is also a revolutionary call to cultivate those precious human qualities that today are in danger of extinction.

Our lives are moving so fast. We need to slow down. The Sabbath is one solution. The Sabbath means more than the absence of work. It is not a normal day off, for television and friends. In a word, Shabbat is about holiness.

What exactly is holiness? *Holiness* itself is a slippery term. What does it really mean? We are used to hearing the word in phrases like *holy smoke, holy war,* or, for some of us growing up in the 1960s, *holy batmobile, Robin.*

In religious contexts, *holiness* is often associated with a place, such as a mountain, a tree, or a temple. In fact, it is quite human to identify holiness with space and size. What church or synagogue is holiest? Why, the one with the biggest building, of course! We naturally perceive God in spatial terms. Children often think of God as some big person. As adults, we still fall into speaking of God as "the man upstairs."

Rabbi Abraham Joshua Heschel, a leading Jewish theologian of the twentieth century, wrote a great deal about holiness. But Heschel wasn't interested in holiness in space. Nor did Heschel think that Judaism in its essence celebrates holy space. As Heschel understood, according to the Bible, the first holy object in the world was not a mountain, an altar, or a building, but the seventh day. In a radical departure from the mythical mind-set of its era, the Bible declares that holiness in space will never match the holiness of time.

With this insight, Heschel wrote in his profound and poetic book *The Sabbath*:

> The meaning of the Sabbath is to celebrate time rather than space. Six days a week we live under the tyranny of things of space; on the Sabbath we try to become attuned to holiness in time.... The Sabbaths are our great cathedrals.[4]

For Heschel, the holiness of Shabbat is about saying no to the usual and ever-growing distractions. It is about stopping and seeing the beautiful things in our lives. It is about saying no to the unrelenting technologies that simultaneously seduce and stress us. Shabbat is about creating for ourselves a temporal island of well-being, a harbor in which we can reclaim our humanity and rediscover our center.

Heschel wrote his best seller about Shabbat decades ago, but his words could not be timelier. For us, Shabbat is like a period inserted into an otherwise endless run-on sentence.

Finding the Joy in *No*

It is sad that, for many of us, Shabbat conjures up the abstention but not the joy. There are many positive observances for Shabbat, some of them even involving delicious, high-cholesterol food. Many observances, such as lighting candles, are quite beautiful.

Nevertheless, the key to Sabbath observance is, in fact, learning to say no. Even so, the prohibitions of Shabbat do not eclipse the spiritual side of Shabbat: the joy of not worrying about our to-do list; the pleasure in being at home with our family; the sometimes-rare delight of sharing a meal together.

Traditional Jews have their own list of what not to do on Shabbat. This list is based on Jewish law. For me, as a liberal but serious Jew, there are things I try not to do on Shabbat, but the motivation is more about therapy than theology. I ponder what makes my life crazy and I try to avoid such activities on Shabbat. It's that simple. So I try not to use the phone, check e-mail, handle money, or do errands. These acts for me are the epitome of ordinary time.

You can do this, too. We all have more control than we think. We simply have to establish a new discipline—a new routine—and stick with it. It might take a few weeks before it starts to feel natural. Don't give up too fast. Make Shabbat a discipline in your life. If someone joined a gym and quit after a week because the exercise wasn't working, you'd suggest that she try it for at least a month. The same is true of Shabbat.

Recently, I started using something called a Shabbat box. It is easy to do. You choose a box and, on Friday afternoon (or on another day, if that is your practice), you place in it your cell phone, iPad, laptop, wallet—whatever you need to put in so the Sabbath feels different.

You can also use the Shabbat box to hold all the things you have left undone. Write on a small piece of paper a word or phrase that signifies a particular concern you would like to leave behind. When Shabbat is over, you can open the box, and the concern will still be there waiting for you.

Rabbi Heschel once wrote, "What we are depends on what the Sabbath is to us.... Inner liberty depends on being exempt from the domination of things.... This is our constant problem ... how to live with things and remain independent."[5] Heschel wrote these words in 1951. They are more relevant today than ever.

Making Holiness Our Target

What we are depends on what Shabbat means to us. We need to let Shabbat remind us that we are more than busy people, subservient to the schedules, machines, and pressures of this crazy twenty-first century.

The Dubner Maggid, the famous wandering storyteller of Poland, relates a tale that is helpful in understanding what the Sabbath should mean to us. Many years ago, a nobleman's son was a student at a military academy, and one of the sports in which he was an expert was shooting bull's-eyes. In fact, he had won many gold medals for his marksmanship. After he was awarded his diploma, the young officer rode home on his horse. Passing through a tiny village, he saw a hundred circles drawn on the side of a barn and in the center of each circle was a bullet hole.

The officer was so amazed that he stopped his horse and yelled out, "Who is this expert shot? A hundred perfect bull's-eyes! That's incredible! Even I could not do that!"

Just then, a young boy walking by looked up at the officer on his tall horse and snickered, "Oh, that's Nar, our town fool!"

"I don't care what he is," interrupted the officer. "Whoever can shoot a hundred perfect bull's-eyes must have won every gold medal in the world! I must meet him and shake his hand!"

"Oh no, no, no, you don't understand," laughed the boy. "Nar doesn't draw the circle first and then shoot. He shoots first, and then he draws the circle."

Many of us think of Shabbat observance as way off the mark. But, in fact, Shabbat is a perfect bull's-eye, the answer to the stress, the family tension, the search for intimacy, and the quest for holiness we all want to experience. We need to make observance of the Sabbath our target, our way out of the wilderness, our bridge to holiness, our best hope to retain our human dignity.

2

Keep a Tab on Mission Drift

N ot too long ago, passengers on a regular flight from Detroit to Tri-City Airport—which is situated between the Michigan cities of Saginaw, Bay City, and Midland—must have felt more than a little confused during a flight attendant's greeting. Obviously not familiar with the area, she welcomed everyone warmly and stated that the destination would be Midland. A few concerned passengers alerted her to the mistake, so she quickly corrected herself by saying they were headed to Bay City. Chuckles rippled along the aisle as she bravely tried again. This time she informed passengers that their destination was Saginaw. Now laughter broke out. At that point, another voice came over the intercom and rescued her. "I'm your pilot, folks," said the voice, "and don't worry—I know where we're going!"

I think we'd all agree that it's nice when someone knows the way. The question is: Do we?

We cannot depend on others for the most important answers about our lives. People can help, but no one else can decide what is best for us. No one else can steer us on our path. At times, we need to find our "inner pilot" so we will set the right direction for ourselves.

Why don't we hear that voice more often? You know the answer: We have too much going on. Consider the story about the young boy and his bank. The little boy's father had just given him a silver dollar to put into his bank. He excitedly ran off to his room to deposit the coin. However, in a few minutes he returned and handed the silver coin back to his father. "Daddy," he said sadly, "here's your dollar back. I can't get it into my bank."

"Why not?" his concerned father asked.

"It's too full," he said, obviously disappointed.

His father accompanied him back to his room and, sure enough, his bank was too full to accept even one more coin. It was stuffed with pennies.

Is your life like that bank—so full of errands, obligations, activities, alarms, e-mail alerts, and text messages that don't really matter? Do you close yourself off from what is truly important—the silver dollars? I think you know the answer.

What Are You All About?

If you're like most people, foremost among the activities you put aside is considering your purpose: why you are here and the actions you take to fulfill your purpose. The very essence of *tzimtzum* is to consider who you are so you can decide what to do and what not to do. If you are to live by your values, you need to set aside much more time for such introspection.

So I ask you: Who do you really want to be in the world? What are the values that you most cherish and wish to nurture in yourself? What must you do to best promote these values? And what are things that keep you from embracing this vision of your higher self?

Henry David Thoreau once observed that "in the long run people hit only what they aim at."[1] I believe he is right. The question is not "Where are you now?" as much as it is "What are you aiming for?"

Are you aiming for the most stuff? If that is the case, then I have news for you. You will never be happy because stuff is never enough. The point of life is not to amass more shoes or clothes than everyone else. Actually, a study released recently states that a household income of $75,000 a year helps bring happiness. Any amount over that does not add any more happiness.

Are you aiming for a sense of oblivion, some Eden-like existence where you are only in the here and now? Some mystics crave this, but this, too, is not a Jewish ideal. As strange as it may sound, Jewish thought pays little attention to inner tranquility and peace of mind. Our path, our direction, isn't about finding serenity or closure.

So what *is* it about?

Well, I hope it's about being a compassionate person, in touch with the needs of others and dedicated to making this world a better place. It's about doing our chosen work a little better. It's about loving our family just a little more. It's about having integrity, having a good name. It's about being a mensch. And I think most of us would agree that we can all do a better job in the fine art of being human.

Staying True to Your Slogan

Successful corporations know they have to labor tirelessly to remind their employees and customers of their mission. They deal with this challenge, in part, by creating slogans that capture the essence of who they are.

For instance, consider these classics:

The real thing (Coca Cola)

The Uncola (7-Up)

Good to the last drop (Maxwell House coffee)

All the news that's fit to print (*New York Times*)

The most trusted name in news (CNN)

Let your fingers do the walking (Yellow Pages)

It's not TV; it's HBO (HBO)

Keeps going and going and going (Energizer batteries)

Think different (Apple computers)

Just do it (Nike)

It takes a licking and keeps on ticking (Timex watches)

There are some things money can't buy; for everything else, there's MasterCard (MasterCard)

It's everywhere you want to be (VISA)

We love to see you smile (McDonald's)

Where's the beef? (Wendy's restaurants)

Some of these are better than others, but they all try to capture the essence of what these companies do, what each one's mission is. So my question is: What is yours? And, just as important, is there a gap between your slogan and your reality?

Wouldn't it be interesting to ponder what your slogan might be? Wouldn't you like to know if you are living up to those words? Remember, even companies and people with stated missions and actual practices sometimes veer away from their mission.

Here's another borrowed term for us to consider: *mission drift*. *Mission drift* is what happens when you forget your purpose and go off in search of something else. First used by the military, the phrase implies that you have let the passion of your purpose be hijacked by other concerns. It happens all the time.

A couple of years ago, Starbucks Coffee was seriously drifting from its mission. The stock was down and the corporation was listing. Howard Schultz, the former CEO, was brought back in to repair the damage. He began by famously closing all Starbucks for three and a half hours to enable the entire staff to be reminded of the core of their business. Many shareholders thought he was crazy. He also gathered ten thousand store managers at a conference in New Orleans—at company expense—to drive home the core mission of Starbucks. Schultz successfully turned the company around not by cutting costs alone or reducing the quality of the coffee. He did so by reminding everyone about the true nature of their business. As he declared, "You can't get out of this [crisis] by trying to navigate with a different road map, one that isn't true to yourself. You have to be authentic, you have to be true, and you have to believe in your heart that this [return to your mission] is going to work. Someone once said to me, 'You are roasting 400 million pounds of coffee a year. If you reduce the quality by 5 percent, no one would know. That's a few hundred million dollars!'" Concluded Schultz, "We would never do that."[2]

This lesson is important. If you want to be authentic, you have to believe in your heart that you have a mission, a plan, and that it will take you where you need to go. But, as the saying goes, you can't have it all, so you have to decide where to focus and what you can let go by the boards.

Finding Your Focus

So where are you going? What are you choosing to relinquish—or, in Schultz's case, not relinquish—so that you can accomplish what matters most?

Clayton Christensen, a professor at Harvard Business School as well as a widely admired author, recently delivered a commencement address. He advised students to invest a lot of time when they are young in finding a clear purpose for their lives. "When I was a Rhodes scholar," he recalled, "I was in a very demanding academic program, trying to cram an extra year's worth of work into my time at Oxford. I decided to spend an hour every night reading, thinking, and praying about why God put me on this Earth."

Continued Christensen, "That was a very challenging commitment to keep, because every hour I spent doing that, I wasn't studying applied econometrics. I was conflicted about whether I could really afford to take that time away from my studies, but I stuck with it—and ultimately figured out the purpose of my life."[3]

The professor went on to note that once you have come up with an overall purpose, you have to make decisions about allocating your time, energy, and talents. Of course, many people with a driving need for high achievement commonly misallocate their resources. For instance, if they have a spare half-hour, they devote it to things that will yield tangible and near-term results. These almost invariably involve something at work—closing a sale, finishing a paper.

Of course, investing time and energy in your relationships with your spouse and children typically doesn't offer that same immediate sense of achievement, and therefore these things—the important things—often get short shrift.

How do you keep your mind on what matters most? A personal mission statement is a good idea, because writing one calls for you to take the time to reflect on your values. But I have also been thinking about a statement that sounds almost like a Zen koan, or riddle, but actually it is a great reminder of the high cost of living a life of purpose: The essence of strategy is denial. This statement was first introduced to me by Dinah Jacobs from the Jewish Leaders Institute at Northwestern University, who has helped American rabbis learn the secrets of business leadership.

What does this mean? To live a life of purpose, you have to spend a great deal of time examining what you should *not* be doing. This does not mean you become a naysayer or a person who does not help others. It implies that you are careful with your time and resources. You can only do so much, and saying no to many things will help you do some things—the most important things—really well.

I invite you to make a list of the things you hold most dear, as well as a list of everything else. Then ponder the wisdom and discipline of these words: The essence of strategy is denial.

When you start saying no to more things, you can say yes more often to what truly matters. Consider this list:

Less TV, more reading

Less shopping, more time spent outdoors

Less clutter, more space

Less rush, more slowness

Less consuming, more creating

Less junk, more real food

Less busywork, more impact

Less driving, more walking

Less noise, more solitude

Remember: Before you can say yes, you have to learn to say no more often.

3

Let Go of Resentment

The Hasidic rabbi Elimelech of Lizensk was once asked by a disciple how a person should pray for forgiveness. The teacher told the student to observe the behavior of a certain innkeeper before Yom Kippur.

The disciple took lodging at the inn and observed the proprietor for several days, but could see nothing relevant to his quest. Then, on the night before Yom Kippur, he saw the innkeeper open two large ledgers. From the first book he read off a list of all the sins he had committed throughout the past year. When he was finished, he opened the second book and proceeded to recite all the bad things that had happened to him during the past year. When he had finished reading both books, he lifted his eyes to heaven and said, "Dear God, it is true that I have sinned against You. But You have done many distressful things to me, too. However, we are now beginning a new year. Let us wipe the slate clean. I will forgive You, and You forgive me."

Can we learn to forgive God? Obviously, such forgiveness may be difficult, especially if our lives have been filled with suffering. But when it comes to God, we are taught that such forgiveness is possible and we hope to have our burdens eased by our mutual forgiveness with God.

If only we could forgive each other in a similar way. Unfortunately, when it comes to other human beings, such forgiveness often seems impossible to achieve. When it comes to the pain another has caused us, there simply is no such thing as unconditional forgiveness. All of us have names and faces of individuals we are not able to forgive. For instance:

- How can we forgive a relative who molested us?

- How can we forgive an ex-spouse who maligns us?

- How can we forgive a thief who has stolen precious memories from us?

- How can we forgive a murderer who has taken a loved one from us?

- How can we forgive a corporation that uses our talents and then discards us?

- How can we forgive a parent who abandons us?

- How can we forgive stupidity, hatred, bigotry, cruelty, and greed?

One of the tragic things about life is that, sooner or later, people will hurt us and we will find ourselves wondering whether or not we can forgive them. We will ponder how we can forgive those who have wronged us, insulted us, those whom we swore we would never speak to again.

On the one hand, we may feel we have no need to forgive. Indeed, those who have hurt us may not be asking for our forgiveness. They may not even know they have hurt us. They may not even still be alive. On the other hand, we also know that without forgiving those who have hurt us, we ourselves may carry a burden so heavy that every day is filled with needless pain and suffering. And we wonder: If we can forgive those who have hurt us, will this pain go away? Will we be relieved of the constant drain on our emotions?

One thing I do know: Nothing destroys a relationship or threatens our well-being faster than resentment. It is the cancer of our emotions. It is the poison of our spiritual life. The word *resentment* literally means "feeling again," and it therefore emphasizes a clinging to our past. Its meaning focuses on those who have hurt us and returning, over and over again, to this vision of our being victims. If we are honest, most of us will admit that we don't want such baggage with us throughout our lives. But how do we let go of our resentment? How do we forgive?

A Focus on Forgiveness

It may help to remember that forgiveness, although difficult, can work in relieving us of resentment. Donald McCullough, a pastor and author, once observed that forgiveness is like an antibiotic, "very rare and almost always effective, that saves relationships from death."[1] Of course, we won't want to use this medicine every day. It's not necessary to forgive most of the people who irritate us. Instead, we simply should learn not to let them bother us so much. We should learn to overlook the petty annoyances they cause and the frustrations they bring to our lives. For instance, the shopper in front of us in the express lane who has fifteen items instead of ten, or the channel-surfing spouse—their actions may be annoying, but they don't require forgiveness. Genuine forgiveness should be reserved for those who really hurt us. Forgiveness is for the deep and searing pain that involves betrayal, disloyalty, or even brutality. One sign of wisdom is learning to know the difference between meaningless irritations and devastating pain.

The Obstacles to Forgiveness

When it comes to forgiveness, even when true pain is involved, there is a fairly simple method to help you accomplish this most difficult task. The trick is to identify the obstacles in your way and then try to overcome them. Such work may not be easy, but it can be effective.

The first obstacle to forgiveness is the perverse pleasure we find in not forgiving someone. Consider the story of a man who had too much to drink at a party, made a fool of himself, and then passed out. He was very remorseful and asked his wife to forgive him. She said she understood and that she would forgive and forget. However, as the months went by, she would refer to the incident from time to time. After a while, he became tired of hearing about it. "I thought you said you were going to forgive and forget," he said.

"I have forgiven and forgotten." she said, "But I just don't want you to forget that I have forgiven and forgotten."

Being human, it's all too easy to cling to our resentment. Unfortunately, the anger and pain we feel can hurt us more than the one who caused it in the first place. Contemporary writer and philosopher Frederick Buechner compares such anger to gnawing on a bone. There's always a little more marrow, just a little bit left, and you keep gnawing on it. The only problem, Buechner points out, is that the bone you're gnawing on is you. A crucial component to forgiveness is deciding if the anger is a delicacy you would like to forgo.

Another obstacle to forgiveness is that often we don't understand what forgiveness really means. For instance, we tend to confuse forgiving with forgetting, but they are not the same thing. There are times when we will forgive those who hurt us, even though we cannot forget. Forgiveness is not saying, "I don't feel the pain anymore." Forgiveness is saying to the one who hurt us, "I do not feel the need to hold on to your involvement in my pain anymore."

Forgiveness is not forgetting; forgiveness is choosing not to actively remember. It's like the time a certain woman, known to hold no resentment against anyone, was asked to recall a particularly cruel thing that had happened to her years before. The woman claimed not to remember the incident, but her friend persisted. "Don't you remember the wrong that was done to you?" To which the woman responded, "No, I distinctly remember forgetting that."

It's also important to note that forgiveness doesn't mean condoning an action. You don't have to tolerate what someone has done to you in order to forgive him. Forgiveness is not saying to the person who has hurt you, "You're okay." Forgiveness is saying, "I'm okay, and I am willing to let God deal with whether you're okay." If you're not okay, you actively look into how you can become okay. In other words, you can forgive someone and still not approve of his behavior. You can forgive him and still refuse to accept what he has done to you. At its core, forgiving is not about the people who have hurt us. Forgiveness is about healing ourselves after we have been hurt.

An additional obstacle to our forgiving—perhaps the biggest one of all—is that forgiveness offends the rational mind. If we think about it, this makes perfect sense. When someone wounds us, when someone has stolen something—or someone—from us, there is no reason why we should let that offense go. There is no reason why we should find compassion in our hearts for the perpetrator of these crimes. But the fact that we can find no rationale for forgiveness doesn't necessarily mean we should not forgive. It may mean we should simply stop being rational.

Or, perhaps, it is better to say that we should be rational and thereby "play out" what happens if we do not forgive. What kind of person or what kind of society do we become if we allow the search for vengeance to consume our lives? Consider the story of Bud Welch. His twenty-three-year-old daughter Julie died in the bombing of the Murrah Federal Building in Oklahoma City in 1995. Here's a statement he made prior to the 2001 execution of Timothy McVeigh, the man responsible for that bombing.

> The first month after the bombing, I didn't even want Tim McVeigh or Terry Nichols to even have trials. I simply wanted them fried. And then I finally come to realize that the reason that Julie and 167 others were dead is because of vengeance and rage. And when we take him out of his cage to kill him, it's going to be the same thing. We will keep the circle of violence going. Number 169 dead is not going to help the family members of the first 168.[2]

In essence, finding ways to forgive may seem like a terrible choice, but consider the upshot of not forgiving.

Stephanie Dowrick, author of *Forgiveness and Other Acts of Love,* suggests that to find our way to forgiveness, we may need to momentarily circumvent the rational mind, even though this is not easy. It means saying to the one who has offended us:

> I will attempt to go on loving the life in you, or the divine in you, or the soul in you, even when I totally abhor what you have done or what you stand for. What's more, I will attempt to see you as my equal, and your life as having equal value to my own, even when I despise what you do and everything you stand for.[3]

Obviously such an approach is difficult to maintain in the face of understandable resentment. "In emotional terms, it is Everest without oxygen, Wimbledon without a racket, La Scala without a score."[4]

Such a challenge would frighten anyone. But it's necessary, for without giving up the resentment—even when such anger is reasonable—we can never free ourselves from the pain and suffering that we do not deserve.

Moving On with "Magic Eyes"

Let me share with you a story that reflects this irrational forgiveness. It's about a baker in a small village who lived a very righteous, upright life. His righteousness was so pure that it was hard to be around him. People respected him but found it difficult to love him. His wife was another matter. She loved people, and while she respected her husband's righteousness, there was an emptiness in her heart.

One morning, after working since dawn to bake his bread, the man came home and found his wife in bed with another man. Although the woman's adultery became the talk of the town, the baker didn't divorce her. He felt that the righteous thing to do was forgive her. Yet in his heart of hearts, he couldn't forgive his wife for the shame she had brought to his name. He let her live with him, but he hated her for what she had done to him. He only pretended to forgive her so he could punish her with his righteous mercy.

The baker's duplicity was recognized in heaven. Each time he would feel the secret hate for his wife, an angel came to him and dropped a small pebble into his heart. And each time a pebble was dropped there, the baker felt a stab of pain like the pain he felt on the day he discovered his wife and her sin. This made him hate her even more. His hate brought him pain, and his pain brought him hate.

The pebbles multiplied and the baker's heart grew heavier and heavier with their weight. There were times when he wished he were dead.

Then one night the angel with the pebbles told the baker how he could eradicate the pain. The remedy was the "miracle of the magic eyes." He would need eyes that could look back to the beginning of his pain and see his wife not as a woman who betrayed him, but as a weak and lonely woman who needed his help. Only by looking at the world in this new way could he heal from the wounds of the past.

The baker complained, "Nothing can change the past. She is guilty, and not even an angel can change that." The angel replied to the baker, "You can't change the past. You can only heal the hurt that comes to you from the past. And you can only heal it with the vision of the magic eyes." The angel then told the baker how to have this vision: He simply had to try to see his wife in this new light. And every time he tried, a pebble would be lifted from his aching heart.

The baker tried to see the world with these new eyes. It took some time, but eventually the pebbles were removed. The baker's heart grew lighter, and he was able to invite his wife into his heart again.

There's nothing logical about the baker's choice, except for the fact that he was tired of the pain and his forgiveness ended the pain. This is the true meaning of forgiveness. We do not pardon the one who has hurt us. We simply decide to move on. We move on because

life is too rich and wonderful to waste on the negative feelings of anger
and resentment that may be our right to own, but also will never let
us be healed. So we bid them good-bye, not because those who hurt
us deserve this grace, but because we deserve it. In short, as Rabbi
Harold Kushner has observed, we get even by letting go. Ultimately,
forgiveness is about refusing to let our resentment rent any more space
in our minds.

Consider this: There is a place in Death Valley known as Dante's
View. From this perch, you have a choice. You can either look down
200 feet to the lowest spot in the continental United States, a place
called Black Water. Or you can look up 14,500 feet and see Mt. Whit-
ney, the highest peak in the continental United States. From this one
spot, you can choose to feast your eyes on the highest or on the lowest.
It's your choice.

4

Downsize!

I enjoy a good paradox. For instance, consider these classics:

Why is the third hand on the watch called the second hand?

Why do *slow down* and *slow up* mean the same thing?

Why do "tug" boats push their barges?

Why do we sing, "Take me out to the ball game" when we are already there?

Why are they called "stands" when they are made for sitting?

Why is it called "after dark" when it is really "after light"?

Why do we put suits in garment bags and garments in a suitcase?

On a more serious note: America is the richest, most powerful nation on Earth, yet we are also the most anxious and spiritually insecure nation on Earth.

In his book *The Progress Paradox,* Gregg Easterbrook asks us to imagine that our great-great-grandparents suddenly materialized in the United States in the present day. What would they think? Of course, they would be awed by the scale and clamor of present-day life. The speed at which we travel would be inconceivable to them. Mid-nineteenth-century physicians urged passengers to avoid railroad trains because they reasoned that anyone moving so rapidly would surely suffocate. Now much greater speeds go unnoticed.

Surely there are things that would distress our ancestors—nuclear bombs, global terrorism, the crassness of our culture. It would be understandable if they demanded in disgust to return to their own time.

But upon further thought, surely they would begin to appreciate the amazing strides that the future has brought. What we take for granted would dazzle them. One hundred years ago, the average American life span was forty-one years. Now it is approaching eighty. The diseases that killed countless people back then are now cured by a few doses of inexpensive medicine. The instantaneous global communication, the effortless living, the unimaginable advances in political freedom, the personal autonomy never known to human beings before—it would be enough to make our ancestors declare that they had arrived at the gates of the Garden of Eden.

There is only one problem with this picture. Despite all the advances, even with all these comforts and miracles, Americans not only are not happier than they were 150 years ago, but they actually think things are getting worse! Americans are better off than ever and they are not a bit happier because of it.

The Paradox of More

What is going on and what can we do about it? Well, the first thing is to recognize a paradox when we see it. When it comes to paradoxes, this one is as good as it gets: The more we acquire, the less content we are. "*Marbeh n'chasim, marbeh d'agah*," declares the Talmud: "The more possessions, the more worry."[1]

What can we do about this gap between what we have and how we feel? Is there a Jewish perspective that can help us reconcile this contradiction? How might we learn to appreciate what we already have without always thinking about obtaining more?

A few years ago, I read a poem about the paradoxes of our age. Included was this reflection: "The paradox of our time in history is that ... we spend more, but have less, we buy more, but enjoy it less."[2] The catch-22 of the more-is-better philosophy is expressed best this way: If more is better, then there can never be a sense of enough, no matter how much more one has, for there is always more needed to make life better.

Statistics support this line of thinking. In 1958, when economist John Kenneth Galbraith appropriately described the United States as the "affluent society," 9.5 percent of U.S. households had air conditioning, about 4 percent had dishwashers, and fewer than 15 percent had more than one car. By 1980 everything had changed. Ronald Reagan successfully beat Jimmy Carter due, in part, to the widespread sense that people were suffering economically, but here's the thing: The percentage of homes with air conditioning had quintupled, the percentage with dishwashers had increased more than 700 percent, and the percentage of households with two or more cars had nearly tripled.

People were far more materially blessed in 1980 than in 1958. Yet despite the astounding economic growth—despite owning more gadgets, machines, and appliances, thought to constitute the "good life"—polls showed that Americans felt significantly less well off than they had twenty-two years before.

The Weight of Comparison

This trend has only gotten worse. We are richer than ever before, but we are not happier. Why not? It could be a matter of perspective. Or, more precisely, it could all be relative. The writer and social commentator H. L. Mencken once defined a wealthy man as one who earns $100 a year more than his wife's sister's husband. A recent study found striking support for Mencken's definition. This study examined the behavior of a large sample of pairs of American sisters, each containing a sister who did not work outside the home. The goal was to learn what factors might influence the other sister to seek paid employment. They considered all the things that are supposed to affect the decision to work—the unemployment rate in the local labor market, the wage rate, education. All these factors had some impact, but relative income was the most powerful: a woman in their sample was twenty-five times more likely to seek paid employment if her sister's husband earned more than her own.

It seems that our ability to enjoy what we have is significantly based on how we compare ourselves to others in our circle. All too often, this need to keep up with the in-laws means that middle-income families, whose inflation-adjusted incomes are no higher now than in the 1970s, have been saving at much lower rates than before, if indeed at all. They're also carrying record levels of credit-card debt and other loans, digging themselves deeper and deeper in debt, largely because they are trying to keep up with a living standard they cannot afford.

The worst part is that such expenditures will never satisfy us. No matter what we buy, there is always something out there that makes us want more. Jewish tradition has recognized the sad fact that acquiring things will never make us happy. The Talmud tells us that, human nature being what it is, the moment a person acquires one hundred he immediately sets his sights on acquiring two hundred. Such is the attraction of possessions; instead of satisfying us, they drive us to desire even more.

Of course, even if we can afford what we have, we are often frustrated by our possessions. We invest a great amount of money in taking care of our purchases. Some might even wonder if we own our possessions or if our possessions own us. Just ask any boat enthusiast.

"Marbeh n'chasim, marbeh d'agah," declares the Talmud: "The more possessions, the more worry."

I can personally attest to this fact. Not too long ago I had a very bad week: In the course of three days, my iPod, my bicycle, and my car all broke down. The amount of aggravation I felt was far greater than the amount of joy such things give me when they are working. I also bought a new car a couple of months ago and you would think that would be great. But I obsess over the tiniest scratch. What is the point of having cool things if our perspective does not allow us to enjoy them?

Blinded by Abundance

Another reason we are not happier, beyond comparing ourselves to others and worrying about what we own, is our general sense of entitlement. In fact, those born between 1977 and 1994 are even given a label: the Entitlement Generation. These are people who have had it all—their own cell phones, cars, everything. Such abundance corrupts.

This is nothing new. In his farewell address to the Israelites, before he goes off to die, Moses prophesies that the Israelites will prosper heartily in Canaan, the new land they are about to enter. The dying leader warns, however, that affluence breeds a distinct mentality that is to be cautiously guarded against.

> Take care lest you forget the Eternal your God by not obeying God's commandments ...; lest when you have eaten and are satisfied and have built fine homes and have dwelt in them; and when your flocks and herds multiply and your gold and silver increases ...; your heart will be lifted up and you will forget the God who brought you out of the land of Egypt, out of the house of bondage. (Deuteronomy 8:11–14)[3]

Moses thus correlates prosperity with forgetfulness of God, wealth with irreligiosity. But why would Moses view the abandonment of religion as a consequence of material success? Is it not foreign to our religious thinking to deny people the right to the fruits of their labor? Indeed, nowhere in our sacred literature do we find the possession of material goods, per se, to be considered an evil.

But isn't this the point? Moses does not condemn prosperity. He condemns the attitude that usually accompanies prosperity. "You will begin to say in your heart," says Moses, "my power and the might of my own hand have won this wealth for me" (Deuteronomy 8:17). You start to think, "Hey, I deserve this!"

This attitude of entitlement never makes us happy. It also isn't good for others. There is an old Jewish story about a rabbi who visits a miser to try to convince him to give to the poor. He asks the miser to look out the window and see the poor people on the street. Then he picks up a mirror and asks the rich man to tell him what he sees. "I see myself," says the miser. The rabbi responds, "Yes. The silver in the mirror reflects back on you but it also keeps you from seeing the world as it truly is. Your riches—your silver—does the same thing. It is blinding you to your duty." One of the side effects of affluence is that it provides us with more silver to block out others so that we may concentrate only on ourselves.

Could Less Mean More?

Whether we desire to have more to enhance our status, we experience frustration that possessions brings to us, or we have unwarranted feelings of entitlement wrapped up in our wanting, the things we own have not made us happier. The rush to buy something fades more and more quickly, and we find ourselves in need of a bigger and bigger fix. If we are serious about growing as human beings and feeling more contentment, then we must change our ways.

A healthier approach to understanding wealth is stated in the Talmud by the sage Ben Zoma. He teaches, "Who is rich? The one content with his or her portion" (*Mishnah Avot* 4:1). This wisdom recognizes that human happiness flows from a state of mind, not from an abundance of material possessions. It comes from recognizing that what we have does not equal who we are. It is derived from appreciating that more is often less.

Jewish tradition has addressed this concern through the ages. In the medieval period, some Jewish communities enacted laws limiting excess in dress, food, and festivities in order to decrease competitive ostentation. The simplicity of Jewish burial rites reflects similar concerns and goes all the way back to talmudic times. In the modern era, the kibbutz movement was founded on an ideal of simple living and antimaterialism.

Of course, there is another side to the story. Most American Jews are descendants of immigrants who worked hard at menial jobs in an effort to get their foot in the door, attain the security that America offered, and provide an education for their children. The progression from sweatshop to City College to suburbs is well-known. Often conflicting—even paradoxical—attitudes about money also made the trip to the suburbs.

Jews have become the wealthiest ethnic group in America per capita, but clearly the legacy of centuries of Jewish poverty and oppression is still with us. They leave behind a residue of insecurity, anxiety, and perhaps even some shame about our current state of financial security. The upshot is almost absurd: We would rather speak about sex than about money. Yet we confront a real problem. Our values are skewed. An example in the American Jewish world is the bar mitzvah culture. On the one hand, we have morning services that affirm the values of modesty, humility, and Torah learning. Then we have extravagant parties in the evening that seem to contradict everything affirmed in the morning!

All this leads to one major point: We need to consider how we might make our lives better by having less instead of more. There is a movement afoot in our country called Voluntary Simplicity—the Hebrew term is *histaplut b'me'ut,* contentment with less—and its seven essential principles are worth considering.[4]

1. *Anavah* (humility): The prophet Micah instructs us to walk humbly with God (6:8). This suggests that we might need to contract ourselves and take up less space. Environmentalists talk about minimizing our "ecological footprints." One way to do this is by choosing to live beneath our means. Examples

include eating a vegetarian diet, buying fewer clothes, and living in more modest quarters. Driving a hybrid (electric-gas) car instead of an SUV reduces our ecological footprint by two-thirds. *Anavah* means that we are not entitled to a hugely disproportionate share of the planet's resources, even if we have the wealth to pay for it.

2. *Ho'da'ah* (gratitude): This value is largely absent from our commercial culture. Realizing that what we have is a gift, not an entitlement, is a spiritual discipline. How to begin? Let's throw out our catalogs! Let's take a moment to say a blessing before we eat. We should remember that a blessing is not the means of endowing the ordinary with sanctity; it is rather a means of taking that which is holy—God's gift—and making it suitable for our everyday use. In other words, blessings are how we remember to never take what we enjoy for granted or as our due.

3. *Bal tashchit* (avoiding waste) and *haganat hatevah* (preserving nature): American life is characterized by excess: Our houses, cars, and even our bodies are getting bigger and bigger. If all the world consumed at our level, it would take four planets to meet the demand. We need to find ways to avoid waste in our personal lives by recycling, using less, and being more aware of our consumption in general.

   One way we can avoid waste and preserve nature is to downsize our diets. We are growing more obese every year, and little seems to stem the tide. We are religiously obligated to care for our bodies, and therefore we should take seriously any wisdom that will help. The answer to our weight problem is simple: *We have to eat less.*

   A personal trainer once gave me a very important piece of advice: "You look like you eat, not like you train." That is, as we age, the only way we can keep our bodies at a healthy weight is to learn that we have to say no to large portions of unhealthy food. We cannot "run it off" or depend on fad diets to curtail the damage done by excess eating. There are many tricks to helping us eat less, from using smaller plates (to fool the eye) to eating small meals that include some protein every couple of hours. This will keep us from becoming too hungry and overeating, and it will maintain our metabolism. We can also engage in short interval training and lift more weights with great vigor. Nevertheless, the basic strategy will not change: We have to learn to live with less food. We have to say no to dessert, to French fries, to beer, and to many things that give us pleasure. Even chocolate! Why would we want to punish ourselves with such deprivation? Because what matters most is a healthier body and more energy. (Bragging rights at our high school reunions is a bonus.)

4. *Bitul z'man* (wasting time): The moments of our lives are precious; we don't know how long we will be here. Unlike most of the world, we American Jews by and large have choices about our time. Do we want to work long hours to maintain an opulent lifestyle? Do we want to spend six hours a week shopping, as the average American does? How much time are we willing to spend in a car, running errands and commuting? How do we find time to nurture ourselves, let alone support partners, family, friends, and community?

5. *Tzedek* (justice) and *tikkun olam* (repair of the world): Voluntary Simplicity helps us to free up time and money to devote to these *mitzvot*. We are commanded to give *tzedakah,* which is an obligation, not an option. The standard for giving that is set in the Bible is 10 percent. Our checkbooks would look very different if we met this standard—yet with careful consumption, it might be achievable. At least we could drive up the percentage much closer to 10 percent than it is for most of us today.

   Tzedakah can also be given through divestment of excess stuff that is useful to others. We should learn to give away clothes every time we buy new ones. The traditional morning blessing "Praised are You, God, who clothes the naked" can be said both when acquiring and when giving away clothing.

6. *Kehillah* (commitment to community): In *Bowling Alone,* Robert Putnam highlights the effects of the decline of civic engagement in America: alienation, isolation, even depression. Since his book was published, the trends have only gotten worse. The symbol of the age is the iPod. We buy it and then close off ourselves. The music is great, but what a price we pay! We Jews have a long, powerful tradition of living in community, and we understand the crucial relationship between individual and community. In modern times, community association is voluntary, and Jewish communities must work hard to remain healthy. It helps to establish informal systems of connection within the community, such as attending a regular Shabbat service or study group.

7. *Menuchah* (rest and renewal): Every year, there is an annual effort to highlight overconsumption by turning the Friday after Thanksgiving—traditionally the biggest shopping day of the year—into International Buy Nothing Day. We Jews have inherited a tradition that sponsors one of these days every week! Shabbat, a day of cessation from commercial transaction, is a cornerstone of Jewish life. But Shabbat is not only about avoiding work or not consuming—it is about getting off the economic treadmill and facing each other as people, rather than as economic actors. Shabbat is about deciding for a day to let everything, including ourselves, just be. These fifty-two annual Buy Nothing Days allow us to trade consumption for personal and communal renewal.

I am not asking anyone to adapt all seven ideas at once. Let's begin slowly. As you learn to simplify your life, may the words of this well-known prayer be a guide for you:

Dear God,
Help me
to live content with small means,
to seek elegance rather than luxury,
and refinement rather than fashion,
to be worthy, not respectable, and wealthy, not rich,
to study hard, think quietly, talk gently, act frankly,
to listen to stars and birds, babes and sages, with open heart,
to bear all cheerfully,
do all bravely,
await occasions,
hurry never—
in a word, to let the spiritual, unbidden and unconscious,
grow up through the common.
This is to be my symphony.[5]

5

Be Present—Really Present—in Love

Years ago, when meeting couples I was to marry, I always asked a potentially embarrassing question: "So, how did you meet?" Sometimes the couple met at a bar, and they might be slightly chagrined by this fact. (One couple had no such qualms. The woman saw the guy at a bar, approached, and asked, "Are you [a] single and [b] Jewish?" And that was that!)

These days, when I ask people I am going to marry how they met, the most common answer is either J-Date or E-Harmony. Although the answers are not as interesting, I am grateful that the Internet has brought so many people together. (Since Al Gore supposedly invented the Internet *and* was the role model for Oliver Barrett in the novel *Love Story,* there is a nice symbiosis: The Internet is the real love story!)

Another way that future couples have been meeting: speed dating. Speed dating—if you have been living on Mars—is the polar opposite of the quiet, unassuming first date, where you stroll through the art museum or enjoy a leisurely hour at a coffeehouse. It is also about as romantic and as sexy as a job fair. Nevertheless, at roughly eight dates an hour, it covers lots of territory with speed and efficiency.

Originally designed by a rabbi to help Jewish singles meet, speed dating has become an intercontinental love industry. If you don't know about it, here's how it works: Organizers gather fourteen or sixteen soul-mate-seeking singles for an evening in a synagogue, a church, or even a bar. Participants start by spending a timed seven minutes in a tête-à-tête with one potential date. When the bell rings, each seeker moves on to the next prospect for another seven minutes, and so on, until the evening is over and everyone has chatted up everyone else.

Participants are encouraged to use their seven minutes productively and economically, avoiding trite questions such as "Sooo, where do you work?" or "What kind of car do you drive?" In seven short minutes, you are supposed to discern the essence of the person's life.

How do you find out something meaningful about someone in seven minutes? Actually, it is only three and a half minutes, because half the time is for the partner to find out about you. Therefore, if you have only three and a half minutes to find out who someone really is, there is time to ask only a few good questions. These questions had better be important. You may want to begin with "How do you spend your time"? On the surface, it may look like you're asking about people's hobbies, but you're actually asking about what they love, that is, what they're passionate about.

Determining What You Love

When it comes to a potential lover, one lesson is paramount: Love is shown in action more than in words. Scholars have noted that in the book of Deuteronomy, love is always a verb—an action—never simply an inner emotion. For instance, we love God by following the *mitzvot* and teaching them to our children. Likewise, if we love someone, that love is reflected in our actions, not just our emotions.

A good way to find out how you love is to ask yourself this question often: "Where am I?" That is, how do you actually spend your time? You may say you love your family, for instance, but the proof of your love is in how you spend your time and to what you pay attention.

If you are honest with yourself, this litmus test is foolproof. You can claim to love many things—family, freedom, certain values—but what you really love is reflected in what you do and how often you do it. You may have pictures of your family on your desk at work, but that is not proof of your love.

To put it simply, attention is the physical manifestation of your love. What you pay attention to—this is what you love. What you repeatedly do, you love.

For example, if you keep pushing your children away when they need you, you may have love for them in your heart, you may find joy in their being, but this is not tangible love. Tangible love is about time, not just intention. Look at the focus of your life—this is where your tangible, real love lies.

What is at the center of your life? How do you spend your time? What does your appointment book or online calendar tell you? What does your credit-card statement reveal? How are you dedicating your precious days, hours, and moments? What receives your care and attention? That is the definition of what you love.

Here's a simple way to think of it. We all say we love our pets. But who actually walks the dog? The dog knows who loves her most. To paraphrase the sign on the wall at the old Clinton war room: "It's the walk, stupid."

It is not too late to reevaluate how we spend our time or with whom we spend it. Of course, we have to earn a living, and we have other obligations. But we should not forget that time is passing. If we are not happy about our priorities, now is the time to change.

I know there is a gap between what I love—or more precisely whom I love—and how I actually spend my time. I don't spend enough time with my loved ones. Sometimes the irony is laughable. Once I was so tired that the only thing I could do was watch TV. It was late afternoon and the movie *Field of Dreams* was on. It was at the part where I always cry—and I don't usually cry at movies. Kevin Costner is going to have a catch with his estranged dad. So my son Benjy comes in and guess what? He actually wants to play catch, and I start screaming, "Don't bug me! Can't you see I'm watching Kevin

Costner bond with his dad?" After saying these words, I stopped for a second, looked at my son, and got my mitt. At least for that afternoon, my body was where my love was.

The question of location is especially critical when it comes to marriage. It is clear that many marriages these days often wither from lack of attention. We are quick to express our love to our spouses, but do our actions reflect our words as we age and our interests change?

I'm not saying married folks should be together 24/7. There is something to the old adage "Marry for life, not for lunch." But healthy relationships depend on a critical amount of time together.

When breaking up, some couples say, "We just grew apart; we had nothing in common." Maybe love means finding new things to do together. Remember: What we do is what we love.

The Love in Subtraction

When you realize that what—or whom—you love is reflected by what you do, you are ready for another question: What do you choose *not* to do? In other words, where *aren't* you? What must you give up so you have more time for what is paramount?

Great sculptors like Michelangelo claim that their art lies in taking away enough stone to discover the masterpiece within. This is also true of life. We need to learn to remove what does not matter in order to enjoy the uncovered richness of what does matter.

I would argue that we need to say no more often. Maybe this means reconsidering our priorities. It certainly means that we have to decide what—or who—matters most to us and then protect that love by letting go of what is not so important.

Do you really need to answer the phone during dinner? Must you agree to yet another commitment from work? Do you really need to take that business trip?

The fourteenth-century mystic Meister Eckhart once pointed out, "The spiritual life is not a process of addition, but rather of subtraction." We usually take the opposite approach. We fill up our lives with more to accomplish and more speed, and then wonder why we don't have time for what really matters.

Consider this story: In the house of study, a rabbi came across several yeshiva students playing checkers when they should have been studying Talmud. Embarrassed, they returned immediately to their books.

But the rabbi smiled and told them not to be ashamed, since they should always study the laws of life wherever they find them. So he asked if they knew the three rules of the game of checkers. Obviously, they assumed they knew what they were playing, but none would be so bold as to appear to teach the rabbi.

Therefore, the rabbi, the master of the Talmud, told them the rules of the game of checkers. First, he said, one must not make two moves at once. Second, one may move only forward, not backward. And third, when one has reached the last row, he may move wherever he likes. Such, he said, is what the Torah teaches. And he left.

Only much later did the students grasp what they had been taught that day: that they should not clutter their lives with more than one move at a time, that they should always keep the goal toward which they pressed in view, and, as they moved to the last row, this goal involved loving others by serving others. True freedom comes from tying ourselves to the needs of others.

This advice would serve us well as we seek to unclutter our lives and reserve our energies so that we may focus on what really matters. Part of growing up means realizing that you can't have everything. Some things must be jettisoned. Make sure you keep the right things. I know that refusal is a strange way of saying yes. But when your plate is full and you need to change your priorities, learning to say no is essential. Remember what the dog knows—the one who loves her walks her.

The Gift of Presence

There is one more issue to consider: In addition to setting the right priorities in our lives by determining where we need to be and where we don't need to be, we also have to understand the difference between being there for our loved ones and really being there.

We can be physically present without being spiritually present. There's an old High Holy Day reading by Rabbis Harold Kushner and Jack Riemer that challenges us to be more fully present. Here is an excerpt:

> What does it mean to hear?
>
> The persons who attend a concert with their minds on business, hear—but do not really hear.
>
> The persons who listen to the words of their friends or their spouse or their children and do not catch the note of urgency: "Notice me, help me, care about me," hear—but do not really hear.[1]

We all know there is a difference between hearing and really hearing. And there is a difference between being there and really being there. We should really be present for those we love. We should be fully engaged in the moment.

You know what I mean. When we experience genuine presence, we know that we have been seen, heard, and understood. Someone "gets" us. We feel valued. Sadly, many of our encounters with others lack such presence. We are distracted or distant. We can fake presence pretty well. We say "uh-huh" into the phone as a friend recounts her day, all the while checking e-mail, hoping she doesn't hear the telltale click of the keyboard. At a cocktail party, a friend moves his head up and down while scanning the room for someone more important to talk to. We try to do too much and end up doing nothing well. As a result, we move through our lives in a fog, only half aware of what has transpired over the course of each day's conversations.

Many of us practice the art of multitasking although we are not as adept at it as we think we are. We will be sending an e-mail and booking flight reservations, while at the same time speaking on the phone to someone. The polite term for this is *multitasking,* but, in reality, especially for the person on the other end of the phone, what we're really doing is an older word. It's *ignoring.* It's certainly not being really present.

A classic modern Jewish tale of the importance of presence, and the consequences of not being present, is the story of the famous philosopher Martin Buber. One day, as he was busy in his study and immersed in mystical ruminations, a despondent young man came to him to pour out his anguish. Buber listened with half an ear, eager to get back to his work. Unfortunately, the young man left the office still troubled, and the next day he committed suicide.

It is possible that this tragedy led Martin Buber to develop his famous I-Thou philosophy of dialogue. In the I-Thou relationship, we are fully present with the other person. We are really listening and showing our genuine love.

How does the I-Thou relationship translate into action? The next time you want to be present—truly present—for a loved one, tries these three tips:

1. Put other work aside. When speaking to a person on the phone, close folders, books, the Internet connection, and anything else that might distract you.

2. Minimize potential distractions. If you are meeting with someone in the office, shut the door, turn off the phone's ringer, and close the computer. At a public venue, take the nonpower seat—the one that faces the wall rather than the other diners, for example—so that all your concentration can be on the person you are talking with. Avoid looking at your watch.

3. Focus your body. Musicians and artists know that posture counts. So should artists of being in the present. When listening to a loved one, turn your body toward the person you are speaking with. Lean forward. Keep your hands and arms in an open position.

Such directions will help us be present when our loved ones need us. Being fully present is how we should express our love.

Here is a tragic and miraculous story about presence. On August 16, 1987, Northwest Airlines flight 225 crashed just after taking off from the Detroit airport, killing 155 people.

One survived—a four-year-old girl from Tempe, Arizona, named Cecelia.

News accounts say that when rescuers found Cecelia, they did not believe she had been on the plane. Investigators first assumed that Cecelia had been a passenger in one of the cars on the highway onto which the airliner crashed. But when the passenger manifest for the flight was checked, there was Cecelia's name.

It is speculated that Cecelia survived because, even as the plane was falling, Cecelia's mother, Paula, unbuckled her own seat belt, got down on her knees in front of her daughter, wrapped her arms and body around Cecelia, and would not let her go.

Nothing could separate that child from her parent's love—neither tragedy nor disaster, neither the fall nor the flames that followed, neither height nor depth, neither life nor death. That's love! That's presence.

To answer the question of how to love in one sentence: We show our love best not by gifts but by presence.

Remember what the dog knows—the one who loves her walks her.

I know that we want to love. We want to be loved, too. But real love takes hard work. Real love takes showing up. It takes compromise. It takes giving up some of who we are so we can share our lives with someone else. It means making choices.

But isn't the reward worth it?

6

Respond to the Right Questions

I believe that questions give us a lot more information than answers. Why? Because questions frame our outlook on the world. There is an old saying that if all you have is a hammer, every problem looks like a nail. In other words, our view of the world is based on the questions we ask. In this case, how can I best use my hammer?

I think that fine literature often conveys its essential message by the questions it poses, often at the opening of the text. For instance, at the beginning of Shakespeare's *Hamlet,* we find the question "Who is there?" If you think about it, isn't the whole question of the play "Is there justice? Does anyone care?"

The first question in the Torah is much like that. In Genesis 3:9, God asks Adam and Eve, after they have disobeyed, "Where are you?" God certainly knew physically where they were, so this must have been a spiritual question, namely, "Who are you?" That is, "What prompted your disobedience of Me? What are your values?"

There is a Hasidic tale, retold by Martin Buber, in which a revered rabbi is falsely accused of crimes against the Russian state and put in prison. His jailer gathers that this is a learned man, and one day he asks the rabbi why God would not know the location of Adam and Eve. The rabbi responds that this question is an existential one and is addressed to all human beings, including the jailer (whose name and age he seems to know without ever having been told). The jailer is chilled to the bone, although he puts on a game face. He understands that the question of Adam and Eve is also asked of him.[1] It is asked of you, too: Who are you? What are your values?

My favorite question in sacred literature is in the rabbinic work called *Midrash Genesis Rabbah*, an early fifth-century interpretation of the book of Genesis. The ancient Rabbis wondered why Abraham was chosen by God to be, more or less, the first Jew. What made him deserving of this singular honor? The Hebrew Bible is silent on this matter. The Rabbis imagine that Abraham is like a traveler who comes to town and sees a building on fire. The traveler asks, "Does anyone care that this building is in flames?" At that moment the owner of the building looks down from an upper level and says that he cares but that he needs help extinguishing the fire.[2] The midrash suggests that Abraham is akin to the traveler, wondering if anyone cares that the world is burning in injustice. And God, from inside the burning building, says yes, but that Abraham—and all humanity—must help to put out the flames.

In the Hebrew version of this story, the word used for building, *birah,* refers to a poorly maintained multistory residential building, an ancient Roman version of a tenement. By placing God on the upper floor, there is the distinct lesson that God is helpless to address the injustices of the world (including maltreatment of the poor). God needs us, and Abraham was the first person to ask if God cares. From this we learn that God chose Abraham because he did something that had never been done before: He asked the right question!

As we seek to focus our lives on what matters most, there is nothing more important than asking the right questions. Indeed, it can be argued that most problems in life come not because we have the wrong strategy but because we have the wrong questions in mind. Our children grow up thinking the question to address is "Which college should I attend?" instead of "How can I live a fulfilling and worthy life?" Or a corporate executive focuses on the question "How can we make more profit for our shareholders?" instead of "How can we make a product that will meet the needs of the consumer?"

In his book *Leadership without Easy Answers,* Harvard professor Ron Heifetz argues that we will be better leaders if we ask the right questions.

Earn It!

I believe that there are many good questions in life, but one is more important than all the rest. God gave us life, and the question we need to ask is "How do we respond?"

Remember the Steven Spielberg movie *Saving Private Ryan*? A crucial scene in the film continues to haunt me. It's at the end of the movie, when Private James Ryan is comforting the soon-to-die captain who has been sent, along with seven other men, to save the private from near-certain death. In the course of saving the private, almost the entire group of soldiers will die. Earlier in the film, expressing the frustration of sacrificing so many men for the life of one soldier, the captain declares that this Ryan (whom he has yet to find) had better go home and cure some disease or invent a longer-lasting lightbulb or something. In other words, the captain seeks some justification for the special effort made to rescue Private Ryan.

Now, as the captain is dying, but confident that Ryan will be saved, he says to the soldier, "James, earn this. Earn it all." The film then jumps more than fifty years ahead to the present day and shows the aged James Ryan desperately asking his wife if, indeed, his life has justified the sacrifices made for it. "Tell me I've lived a good life," he beseeches. "Tell me I'm a good man."

In a sense, all of us are like Private Ryan, even if our life circumstances are not as dramatic. By being born, all of us are granted the gift of life. From the perspective of our religious tradition, all of us are challenged by the same words that the captain spoke to Private Ryan: Earn this! Live your life in such a way that the gift of life is justified.

Likewise, it is appropriate for each of us to consider these questions: Am I living a good life? Am I a moral human being? Does my life reflect the proper gratitude I require for having been granted the gift of life?

If you think about it, each of us is here on Earth in the face of incredible odds. What if your parents had never met? What if the egg had never been fertilized? What if something had gone wrong during the pregnancy? In my own case, I know that if my older brother had not died as a child, the likelihood of my being born would be almost nil. I also know that my mother's escaping Hitler's Germany was a very unlikely occurrence, not to mention my father surviving the war in Europe, so I don't take my own existence for granted. I feel compelled to live my life in response to the simple but powerful command "Earn this!" I feel compelled to address the question "Am I a good person?"

All of us have read stories of people who miraculously avoided being targets of terror attacks or casualties of tragic accidents. They missed the airplane. They went to work late. Or maybe they were rescued in time. My guess is that these people are asking themselves how they will now live their lives as a reflection of their new gift. They will wonder if they are good enough.

Are you a good person? Naturally, most of us would say yes. You are not a murderer. You are not guilty of heinous crimes. But are you really as good as you could or should be? Does your life reflect enough righteousness, enough goodness? How can you tell? I think it's worth considering the same question Private Ryan must wrestle with every day: Have you earned your right to life? What more might you be doing to justify your existence?

What Is Good?

When it comes to defining goodness, we should begin by clearing up an important point: Being good is not the same as not being bad. In Miami I used to drive by O. J. Simpson's house. At first I would always feel a little smug as I drove by. I would say to myself, "Hey, I may not be perfect, but at least I'm not him," assuming he was, in fact, guilty of killing two people. Of course, when you think about it, such a moral victory is pretty hollow.

It is very easy to feel smug; after all, we are not terrible people. But when we consider the gap between who we are and the goodness we might practice, most of us have little reason to feel satisfied. In the equation posed by *Saving Private Ryan,* it's not enough to "earn" our life by avoiding evil. We must also actively practice being good. Each of us must continue to ask ourselves, "Could I do better? Could I be more sensitive? Could I be more compassionate?"

Having said this, I don't believe that being good means being perfect. For just as there is a danger in setting our ethical standards too low, there is also a danger in setting them too high. In responding to the question "How have I earned my right to life?" by asserting that nothing short of perfection is the answer can all too easily make us feel perpetually guilty. It can lead us to conclude that, no matter what we do, it's never going to be enough. Best-selling author Rabbi Harold Kushner once observed that a lot of misery in the world can be traced to the mistaken notion that we need to be morally perfect for other people—and God—to love us. The problem with this ideal is that, being human, we are bound to fail. Setting ourselves up for failure, we associate the challenge of being good with feelings of failure. If we can never be good enough, why even try?

Worse, we think that if only we were good enough, we wouldn't become sick or have an accident. We mistakenly assign to God the role of some cosmic Santa Claus, rewarding us or punishing us, and when life doesn't work out, we either blame ourselves or blame God.

But life is too complex and nuanced for such thinking. In reality, we are not perfect and we are not in complete control. We will make mistakes, but we need not think of ourselves as terrible people. Jewish tradition does not celebrate perfect people. Picture anyone you want from the Hebrew Bible: Adam and Eve, Abraham and Sarah, Moses, or King David. None of these people was perfect—far from it. But God loved them. Likewise, God doesn't love us because we are saints. God loves us for who we are: frail human beings. What God wants is for us to try our best, not to always succeed. Earning our lives is about trying. When we fail, as we will, God loves us in our contrition, in our brokenness. Indeed, there is nothing more spiritual than a broken person who is willing to admit mistakes and grow from them. Or as a bumper sticker puts it: God Loves You Anyway.

Good Is a Verb

So when it comes to goodness, we find ourselves somewhere in the middle of the spectrum—not aligned with hell, but not in heaven either. Neither morally neutral nor perfect. Therefore, the central question becomes, How do we get as close to perfection as we can, recognizing that we will never actually arrive there? There is a great distance between being morally neutral and being perfect. Somewhere in this expanse lies the border of actually being a good person. This is the place we should seek to reach. But how do we know it when we get there?

Judaism has always emphasized the power of the deed, so maybe the answer lies in what we do. The prophet Isaiah declared that we should "cease to do evil and learn to do good" (1:16–17). But what does *learn to do good* really mean? Clearly good actions are implied. Or to paraphrase Forrest Gump, good is as good does.

This means that in order to be good people, we have to treat others well. We cannot make ourselves the center of our world. An example of such a person in ancient Jewish tradition is Joshua ben Gamla. We are told that whenever his name is mentioned we should add the words *May he be remembered for goodness.* Why does he merit this praise? Joshua ben Gamla took it upon himself to establish a system of public education for Jewish youngsters in ancient Judea, the first of its kind in the world. This education especially benefited orphaned children, who otherwise would have grown up ignorant. Joshua ben

Gamla assumed the responsibility of Torah education for those who could not help themselves. For the Rabbis of the Talmud, such an act reflected the epitome of goodness.

Jumping from the first century to the twenty-first, consider this commencement advice from author Anna Quindlen:

> Care so deeply about ... goodness that you want to spread it around. Take money you would have spent on beers and give it to charity. Work in a soup kitchen. Be a big brother or sister. All of you want to do well. But if you do not do good, too, then doing well will never be enough. It is so easy to waste our lives: our days, our hours, our minutes. It is so easy to take for granted the color of the azaleas, the sheen of the limestone on Fifth Avenue, the color of our kids' eyes, the way the melody in a symphony rises and falls and disappears and rises again. It is so easy to exist instead of live.[3]

I would add that it's so easy to forget our obligation to God for the life we've been given. It's so easy to live with a sense of entitlement, to say, "The world exists because of me." But what we should say is "I exist and therefore I serve the world." Please understand: I don't personally believe in a God who rewards and punishes us. I'm not saying, "Be good or else." The Torah often does say this, but I reject this rationale. What I believe is that God wants us to be good but stands aside and allows us the free will to make our own decisions.

Enjoy and Bring Joy

Using our free will, we should serve each other with genuine kindness and sensitivity. Indeed, we don't just do what is expected of us. We do more. Therapist David Reynolds calls this "walking the second mile."[4] We are asked to walk one mile for someone else's sake; the second mile we walk because we have chosen to do so. It is our way of earning our right to be here. We're asked to serve food in a soup kitchen, but we end up chairing the food shopping committee, too. We're asked to volunteer one hour to help clean up after a neighbor's house has been vandalized. Instead, we work with our neighbor until the cleanup is finished. When we are told to spend an hour with someone we dislike, we spend two hours and try to find something likable in her. In general, we seek ways to give more and expect less.

It's also important for us to find value in giving of ourselves in less direct ways. For instance, consider the story of a woman sitting in the park of an affluent neighborhood, feeding the pigeons. One day she brings with her a whole loaf of fresh bread just to feed her avian companions. Little by little, pinch by pinch, she feeds each pigeon with joy. She sits there without being noticed by anyone in the neighborhood.

Then suddenly a man comes by and decides to confront this woman about her waste of good food. He tells her that she should not throw away fresh bread on a bunch of pigeons that can find food anywhere when there are so many starving people in Africa. To which the woman responds, "Well, I can't throw that far!"

Let's learn from this woman the wisdom of doing good right here at home. Let's meet the challenge of being nicer to our own family and friends.

When we have festivals in Judaism, we are commanded in Hebrew, "*Visamachta*—You shall rejoice." But with a slight revocalization of the word, the ancient Rabbis read it as "*Viseemachta*—You shall cause to rejoice." The purpose of life, then, is not only to enjoy but to bring joy; not only to benefit but to benefit others; to earn our blessings by sharing them with those in need. After all, one way of saying thank-you is to say, "Much obliged"—literally, this means that we are obligated. We are duty-bound to pay back God for our gifts. This is not only theology; it's also good manners!

Private James Ryan understood this truth. I believe all of us can also grasp this equation:

life = gratitude

gratitude = obligation to serve others, to earn our life

It's that simple.

Or as the anonymous poet put it:

> *Your task:*
> *To build a better world, said God.*
> *I answered: How?*
> *The world is such a large, vast place*
> *So complicated now*
> *And I, so small and useless am.*
> *There's nothing I can do.*
> *But God in such great wisdom said:*
> *Just build a better you.*[5]

"Where are you?" asks God. How do you respond?

7

Say No to Loved Ones, Especially Your Children

I n *The Death of the Hired Man* by Robert Frost, a character describes home as a place where "when you go there, they have to take you in." While such a sentiment sounds nice, clearly a home environment does require norms of behavior and boundaries in order for it to be a healthy place. When I counsel engaged couples, it is always interesting to note how they go about determining the boundaries where one of them stops and the other begins. Much of this determination, of course, is a function of the family in which they were raised. My job is to help them see the differences in their upbringing so they will not be so surprised and possibly hurt when they realize that different families have different norms and different boundaries.

Saying no at home is usually more complicated than saying no to friends, but both fall along a spectrum. Ultimately, none of us should accept being part of a hurtful, abusive relationship. John Cheever's elegiac short story "Goodbye, My Brother" catalogs the pain of the narrator as he realizes his sibling will never be the brother he deserves. In his writings, Cheever often returned to his difficult relationship with his actual older brother, Fred. The inability of a sibling to return affection can haunt a sensitive person, so what is one to do? Unfortunately, you reach a point where the only course is to let that person go, to say no to the pain she causes and thereby make room for the people who return your love. The Talmud says that when one divorces the wife of his youth, even the altar [God] sheds tears (*Gittin* 90b). I would add that when any sibling cannot return one's love with affection, God would shed more tears. But sometimes this is the only way.

Knowing When to Say "No More"

I once counseled a woman who was married to a man suffering from bipolar disorder. She felt that her lot in life was to stick by this man, even if he refused to seek help. She reasoned that God must have assigned this fate to her. I suggested another point of view: Try as we might, we cannot save others from themselves. I told her to devise a plan to try to help this man for a certain amount of time and then, if nothing came of it, she had no choice but to leave the marriage. Leaving is never the first choice; sadly, however, sometimes it is the only choice.

Many years ago, Peter Kramer, author of the best-selling *Listening to Prozac,* published a book about relationships, titled *Should You Leave?* Each of us has to answer that question for ourselves, but I believe we should make the decision based on an awareness of our values. If someone related to us by blood or marriage cannot respect those values, there are many reasons to support leaving. Having said that, I always remind people considering divorce that leaving a relationship is akin to playing Scrabble. If you have really bad tiles, it is tempting to skip a turn and exchange all the bad tiles for better ones, hopefully. It always feels good when I do so. The problem is, I have never won a game using that strategy.

Holding Back versus Hovering

You can divorce a spouse, of course. But, sadly, you cannot divorce your child. I say *sadly* because most parents have felt at times a strong desire to do so. Our children cause much misery, as well as a wonderful, albeit too small amount of joy. We cannot divorce them, but we can set limits and refrain from rewarding them for inappropriate behavior.

A great challenge facing parents today is the need to hold back from doing things for their children. The current obsession so many parents have is for their children to get into great colleges, as if this were a sign of assured success. Sadly, when parents hover over their children, (over)filling their schedules with lessons, coaches, and exotic African experiences they can reflect on in their college essays, they forgo the vital opportunity children need to work for the sake of gaining financial independence and—even more simply—to gain experience in problem solving. I fear that we are creating a society of young people who do not know how to succeed in life because they have never been given the opportunity to try and fail. As Wendy Mogel writes in her books on parenting, we do our children a great disservice if we place them in situations in which they cannot learn how to fail. *Tzimt-zum* parenting means we practice the art of letting go, not to encourage them to fail, but so they can learn from their failures. The best thing we can give our children as they grow up and face a challenging world is resilience. If they never learn to fail, how will they acquire resilience?

A few years ago I was taking my younger son, Benjy, to visit colleges. On our way from the University of Michigan in Ann Arbor to the University of Wisconsin in Madison, Benjy announced that he wished to go to Africa that summer, as he believed such a trip would help him with his college applications. While he was suggesting this plan, I had been listening on my Kindle to Wendy Mogel's *The Blessing of a B Minus*. As my son announced his desire, Wendy was explaining that college admissions boards see right through the cynical ploy of spending a small fortune to go to Africa in order to look like a great humanitarian. The only more cynical ploy (possibly) is to have your friend hire your child as a summer intern. (And vice versa, of course.) The real education for children is for them to earn minimum wage and practice the fine art of having to show up and do a job or face being fired. Having consequences is the best life lesson we can share with our children. To create the environments needed for these lessons means parents must practice ceding control. For some reason, this practice seems even more difficult today than ever before. Yet how can our children ever grow up if they know the safety net is always beneath them?

Resilience Involves Role Models

What, exactly, are the obligations of a parent toward a child, according to Judaism? We read in the Talmud (*Kiddushin* 30b):

> The Rabbis taught: A father has these [biblical] obligations to his son: to circumcise him, to redeem him, to teach him Torah, to get him a wife, and to teach him a trade. Some say, also to teach him to swim. Rabbi Judah said, "Anyone who does not teach his son a trade teaches him thievery." Thievery? Really? Rather, "It is as though he teaches him thievery."

The ancient Rabbis understood that if we do not give our children tools for resilience, we are leading them to fail, at best, and to a life of crime, at worst. Swimming is also an important concern—especially for those of us who raised our children in southern Florida, where almost every friend's home has a swimming pool. I would add that parents today also must teach their children to figuratively swim in our contemporary sea of hazy morals and the misplaced worship of celebrity and success.

How do we teach resilience? First we have to be good role models. Children have to learn that we, too, are not perfect and that we, too, struggle. Should parents never argue in front of their children? If we never do, what happens the first time that child has an argument with a significant other? How does someone learn the right way to argue without guidance?

Here's a Hasidic teaching from the Kotzker Rebbe, a nineteenth-century sage:

> A man came to Menahem Mendel of Kotzk and asked how he could make his sons devote themselves to Torah.

Menahem Mendel answered, "If you really want them to do this, then you yourself must spend time studying the Torah, and they will do as you do. Otherwise, they will not devote themselves to the Torah, but only tell their sons to do it. And so it will go on.

"If you, yourself, forget the Torah, your sons will also forget it, only urging their sons to know it, and they will forget the Torah and tell their sons that they should know it. And no one will ever know the Torah."

Not only is the Kotzker Rebbe saying that we should model lifelong learning for our children, he is also reminding us that we teach our children by the choices we make. Ultimately, however, they need to learn to make their own choices. Giving advice to our children is not as effective as helping them learn to brainstorm. After all, we will not always be there with them to work through problems so they need to learn to do it for themselves.

The test—the letting go and saying no—comes when we want to step in and solve the problem, but instead sit back and allow them to think it through on their own. This is not abdication of responsibility, although it may feel that way. It is giving them the gift of resilience. We know they will face significant adversity in life. Our job is to help them learn to navigate through difficult circumstances.

The great jazz musician Miles Davis used to say that if you hit a wrong note in jazz, the important thing is the next note. Either you have a disaster or you have music. It's up to you. I cannot think of anything more important to teach our children. After all, falling in the water is usually not a terrible thing—but only if you know how to swim.

8

Stress Less to
Do More

When I was a fledgling rabbi, an older colleague took me aside and advised me that when the senior rabbi for whom I would be working asked me to do something, his saying *please* should not give me the impression that there was any appropriate answer besides *Yes, sir.* There was wisdom in this remark, in that one should always remember that saying no to the boss is not usually a good idea. Nevertheless, our cultural norms in the United States have been shifting in recent decades, and the definition of who is the boss is also up for renewed consideration.

The clichéd observation "No one ever regrets on his or her deathbed not spending more time at work" is not reflective of the complexity of life today. Many of us find great meaning in our work and, honestly, less satisfaction at home. (I know a CEO who mused that he liked knowing that at work, if he asked nicely, anything would be done, whereas at home his request would most likely be ignored.) The real issue is knowing our values so we do not agree to do anything that goes against them, whatever the context. We must have enough self-confidence to know that we can say no in the appropriate context and still feel good about ourselves.

Refining the Questions

In the last chapter we addressed the challenge of saying no to family. Now we look at the equally difficult, albeit different issue of saying no at work (and hopefully keeping one's job).

Most people think that saying no at work means learning how to do less and thereby avoid (1) doing more than you are being paid to do and (2) failing because you are trying to do too much. Both are understandable goals. However, the essential question is not how to work less, but rather how to define your job in a way that will lead to success without overextending yourself and thereby failing at work or in your private life. I am not speaking of the old-fashioned "gentleman's C," wherein the Yale preppie with a trust fund works just hard enough to get by. I mean that there is a difference between working hard and working with efficiency. The only way to be efficient is to define at the outset the goals you are striving to reach. God knows, we cannot do everything well.

Many years ago, at the synagogue where I serve, we had an executive director who worked sometimes eighteen hours a day and yet was always failing in key areas. I took him to lunch one day and bluntly told him his job was at risk, but I could help him save it. He simply had to go to the board of directors and ask them to prioritize his tasks, thereby giving him direction on how to focus his limited time. The man refused my advice, saying the problem was that the board simply had to cut him "more slack." Today I still do not know what *more slack* means. I do know that his contract was not renewed.

Workplaces change, but human nature is fairly static. People get anxious and do not leave their anxiety at the threshold of their workplace. Colleagues, superiors, and board members will ask many things of you and often will not even be aware of what they are asking. Our job as employees is not to say yes in any situation (unless you serve in the military and then only if they are not Nazis). Our task is to help them refine their request. It's not that we are saying no, per se, but that we are helping them to specify for us what the task is all about.

Recently, the preschool director at our congregation asked our executive committee for a large advertising budget because enrollment was down. The committee said no, not because they did not want to support the school (or the director), but because the advertising solution presupposed that the committee knew what, in this world of changing demographics and parental needs, the preschool was going to be "selling." Instead of approving the advertising budget, the committee appointed a fast-working task force to address the larger question of the preschool's identity. It freed up some resources—in this case, time as opposed to money—to make sure that what matters most, as opposed to what seemed most urgent, was addressed.

I am confident that, no matter what the nature of our work, there are many times that, by taking a step back, we can help our organizations refine the questions they seek to answer so that we make sure we are addressing the right questions. In a world of uncertainty and anxiety, this approach will rarely make us popular. After all, people like to believe in simple solutions, which usually involve spending money or hiring (and firing) people. Making room for what matters most means taking off the table many of the "feel-good" gestures that do not accomplish lasting change or lead to better long-term results.

Think back to the decision of Apple's Steve Jobs to forgo creating a PDA. Jobs faced tremendous pressure to compete with Palm. There had also been a great deal of money and time spent on the project. It took great confidence and insight for Jobs to pull the plug and thereby free up resources for the development of the iPod. In a world where people do not like to hear the word *no*—even from the CEO—the sign of a true leader may be the ability to say no, early and often.

Take Yourself Out of the Game

Another challenge at work, besides learning to say no, is avoiding all the power traps that colleagues devise for each other, be they "triangulation" or engaging in mind games. At heart, the working organization is only a few steps removed from the medieval royal court, where courtiers learned to be deceptive in order to advance their position relative to the king and queen. Today the king and queen have been replaced by the president and CEO, but the rest of the rules have not changed much. Corporations still are pyramids, and your coworkers know that there is only so much room at the top. Nevertheless, most of these power games drain your energy and do not further the goals of the organization. I suggest that you learn about them so you're not fooled by them, and then refuse to play such games.

It's not that we are more righteous than these devious colleagues; it's just that we are too practical and idealistic to bother with these games. We are idealistic because we care about the job we are doing more than the advancement. We are practical because we realize that deceiving others requires energy that can be better spent meeting our professional responsibilities.

Make Room for the Strength of Others

When someone reaches the level of executive in an organization, it is counterintuitive at first to realize that a major part of the job is decid-ing what not to do—what product not to create, what e-mail not to write, what staff person not to confront. It takes great discipline not to respond to the urgent and often emotionally charged task that is tugging at you like a rambunctious puppy. Yet when we practice lead-ership, we are avoiding the "ready, fire, aim" approach so common in organizations today. Stepping back is almost never as satisfying as wading into the fray, but leadership must be about perspective if it is to succeed, and this perspective only comes from distance.

In 1974, *Sh'ma* founding editor Rabbi Eugene Borowitz pub-lished an essay titled "*Tzimtzum*: A Mystic Model for Contempo-rary Leadership." In the essay, Borowitz argued that Jewish leaders (including rabbis) focused too much on success and not enough on the humanity of the people they were leading.[1] Long before *kabbalah* became a buzzword, Borowitz understood that the mystical myth of kabbalah—making space for creation to emerge by voluntary contraction—was a blueprint for leaders to follow: by reining in the exercise of their power, they could allow others to emerge as more fulfilled human beings.

I believe that Dr. Borowitz was prophetic. Our world today is far too complicated to be run by single-minded, power-driven leaders. Leadership today is better served by the model that Dwight D. Eisenhower followed when he became president of the United States. Ike knew how to be a great general, but he didn't possess all the skills needed to be the leader of the free world. Yet he succeeded because he was secure enough to hire people better than him in many different areas and then let them do their jobs.

As a congregational rabbi, I follow that model as well. I have been lucky to engage wonderful staff members, often with greater expertise than I have, and then I let them do their jobs. I do not abdicate responsibility for the work they do, but neither do I micromanage them. The trick is to figure out before you hire someone what strengths you are looking for, and then hire the person who best embodies those strengths. It is also helpful to make sure that the person has the right attitude. In fact, as restaurateur Danny Meyers likes to say, when hiring for a restaurant, attitude matters slightly more than ability because ability can be taught, but you can't teach someone to be a people person.

So, whatever leadership position you find yourself in—and we are all leaders in some way, for leadership is an attitude more than a position—I believe we lead best by letting others play to their strengths.

It is beyond the scope of this book to address the issue of leadership on a major level, such as leadership of the national Jewish community or in American politics, but Harvard professor Ron Heifetz, in his book *Leadership without Easy Answers,* makes the point that Lyndon Johnson was a fine leader when it came to 1960s domestic issues. He knew how to step back and let Congress pass the laws that dramatically addressed the civil rights inequalities of the nation. When it came to foreign policy, however, Johnson tried to control the agenda, and he lost the presidency over it, not to mention continuing a terrible and tragic war.

From this we learn that leadership is about recruiting brilliant people who speak with each other, debate the issues with transparency, and seek to solve problems as collaboratively as possible. It is not about keeping secrets and manipulating others. Such an approach is not only immoral; these days it is also impractical.

Even in the Bible, the notion of a single leader who is above the law is derided. We read in Deuteronomy that if "after you have entered the land ... you decide, 'I will set a king over me, as do all the nations about me,'" the king will not be able to do whatever he wishes. Instead, he shall have a copy of the Torah by his side, and he will read it, so he will be guided by a mission larger than pleasing and protecting himself (17:14–20).

The upshot of this model was not only that the king had checks on his power. The vacuum created by this limit made it necessary to establish a civil service consisting of the Levites and priests. A later development was the rise of the sages (soon to be called Rabbis). The prophets also arose as checks to the authority of the king. In particular, the choice of going to war was not centered on the wishes of the king. He needed the consent of the other leaders (later to be called, collectively, the Sanhedrin).

The Bible presents these developments as happening before Moses gives up his power (also an unusual phenomenon) so that his successor, Joshua, would have a better chance of bringing to fruition the vision of creating a sacred state in the Promised Land. By limiting the power of the king (*tzimtzum*), Moses bequeaths a gift for future generations. His principle still holds true: Spread the power and make leadership about accomplishing the overall mission, not fulfilling personal dreams of glory.

Let's not discount Moses's ceding his position and allowing Joshua to succeed. Many a congregational rabbi has been hampered in his or her job because the retired colleague still hangs on to power, with sometimes nothing more than a well-placed criticism. The biblical ancients, such as Abraham, Jacob, and Moses, took leave of their people with a blessing. This practice reminds us that the final job of a leader is to say thank-you and then leave with grace and class.

Pulling Back Can Mean Better Performance

When we pull back, we allow others to step up and fill the vacuum. Imagine the creativity from others that might surface. Remember that pulling back is not about being passive-aggressive or just plain passive. It is about allowing space for others to rise to the challenge. It has to be planned and executed well, but it will release a wonderful kind of energy. To let go responsibly means to delegate well and to be clear about what you are asking others to do without micromanaging, which is not letting go at all. The best way to do this is to learn what President Eisenhower used to teach: Surround yourself with smarter, better people, and let them do their jobs.

Responsible executives know that the following phrases, when used correctly, are not inappropriate: *I don't know. Can you help me? I was wrong.* This is the practice of *tzimtzum* at the deepest level. It says, "I am not God. I am not omniscient or omnipotent." Think about it like this: Just as God, according to Rabbi Luria, needed to contract in order to make space for human beings, so too do we need to contract our presence at work in order to let other people do their work.

The best part of this approach is that you will stress less and do more.

9

Stop Ignoring Your Mental Garbage

I have always hated meditation, at least until recently. It is not for lack of trying. I would love nothing better than to quiet my busy mind. But when I try to concentrate on my breathing or a certain word, I usually just get bored, think more than ever, or fall asleep. However, thanks to actual training in meditation (like anything else, you need a teacher if you want to do it well), I now realize its power. In fact, I have begun to practice meditation at least a few times a week, for fifteen minutes. By meditation I do not mean relaxation, but mindful focus on one's breath or a simple word, or mantra. That is, I am recommending letting go of conscious thoughts in order to reach the unconscious or, more precisely, letting your unconscious reach you.

Meeting the Thief

Let me share with you a teaching of the founder of Hasidic Judaism, the Baal Shem Tov, also known by the acronym for his name, the Besht. Born in the backwaters of the Carpathian Mountains, located in eighteenth-century Poland (now in Ukraine), the Baal Shem Tov anticipated our own struggles with modernity. At the same time, his teachings are an invitation to delve inward, a map that allows us access to premodern and even prehistoric modes of religiosity, and to the transforming secrets of the Jewish esoteric tradition.

As an engaged mystic, one who is of the world rather than withdrawn from it, the Besht believed that we find God in the ongoing stories of our own lives, and he believed in the value of each individual life. Following his lead, even our struggles are to be seen in the context of the godly. Difficulties do not come from God, but God is part of our struggles with them.

The Baal Shem Tov did not leave behind many teachings, but there are numerous stories told about him. In one example, after he had been teaching for quite some time, his followers asked him, "Rebbe, what is different since you have come and shared your wisdom with us?"

And he replied, "Before I came, when a thief tried to enter the house, the people would shout and scream and try to scare the thief away. Now that I have come, when a thief tries to enter the house, the people lie in wait. They trap the thief, and they hand the thief over to the proper authorities."

Of course, this is not an argument about literal burglaries. Rather, it is a question about the nature of the human soul. The house the Baal Shem Tov speaks of is the conscious mind. In Jungian terms, the thief is our shadow side—our failures, our shortcomings, our embarrassments. It is the stuff we try to keep hidden from our conscious minds. It's not just the things we have done, but also the things we are drawn to do. The thief is the temptation to do evil—our lusts and our temptations to hurt ourselves and others.

The ancient Rabbis saw the thief as the *yetzer hara,* the evil inclination. In Yiddish we might call it the *schmutz,* which basically means an unpleasant unidentified thing (literally, it means "dirt"), as in "Boychick, you have some *schmutz* on your face. What were you eating?"

So, in essence, the Baal Shem Tov is saying to his followers, there was a time when people felt the evil inclination coming upon them, and they would try to scare the evil inclination away. Now, he says, the people let the *schmutz* in, they acknowledge that it can't be scared away, and they deal with it. In other words, they work it out, they own their *schmutz*.

The Baal Shem Tov's wisdom guides us today, encouraging us to own our *schmutz*. By shouting, screaming, and trying to scare away our evil inclination, we display an immature attitude. And it won't work—the thief will duck around the corner and plot another heist. Instead, we are asked to admit that there is something to learn from our evil inclinations, from all our actions—even our failures.

Owning Our *Schmutz*

Mindfulness meditation is a way of preparing the house for the thief to enter. When practicing meditation, we paradoxically quiet our minds but at the same time discover a heightened awareness of how we interact with the world. It is a familiar concept in Eastern spiritual disciplines; both Zen masters and Hasidic rebbes have been teaching it for centuries.

But for our spiritual purposes, mindfulness meditation is more than paying attention to the world. It is specifically about addressing our inner truths, our *schmutz,* and what there is to learn from them.

I have tried mindfulness meditation throughout the years. The basic discipline in meditation is to concentrate on your breath and let your subconscious come to the fore. I always found it hard to do because it's hard for me to let go of my conscious ego. Finally, last year I found myself more successful at the practice, but I was in for a nasty surprise. My meditation did not make me feel relaxed or good. Indeed, it seemed to be bothering me. I felt worse, not better, after meditation.

Then I read *Jewish Meditation Practices for Everyday Life,* Jeff Roth's book on Judaism and meditation, and his words helped me.[1] He observed that mindfulness meditation is often unpleasant, especially when it works. For him, the practice is like revealing all the garbage under the kitchen sink. It stinks. But here's the thing: When you see the garbage, you deal with it. You take it out of the house and you dispose of it. And that's a good thing.

Subconscious garbage can stink up your life. Imagine that it's overflowing the wastebaskets in the various rooms of your home: the kitchen, the bedrooms, the bathrooms, the den, or the workshop. What does your garbage look like? Rotten eggs of plans never hatched? Bones from dreams that died or illicit desires? Tangled strings of frustration? Broken glass and rusty nails of anger? Sad wads of used tissues?

Or maybe the garbage has been lying around for so long that it's no longer even recognizable.

When was the last time you took out—or even acknowledged—your emotional and mental garbage?

Garbage? What Garbage?

This leads us back to the Baal Shem Tov. I think that in the modern world we are worse than the shouters and the screamers of the Baal Shem Tov's parable. We cannot even admit the invasion of the Baal Shem Tov's thief. We would rather pretend that we have no evil inclination, no garbage, no *schmutz*. We would rather pretend that our sins are somehow justifiable, not really anybody's fault, and certainly not our own.

If we start to feel bad about our true selves, we find ways to distract ourselves from this painful truth. We become experts in finding excuses, rationalizations, justifications—anything rather than acknowledging our own shortcomings. We focus on other people's *schmutz;* we see their jealousies, recognize their psychological failings. The last thing we want to do is face our own evil inclination.

Yet mindfulness meditation—when it works—forces us to do just that. It is a controlled way of letting the thief inside to allow us to plod through the jumble of our flagrant disregard, our laziness, and our guilt. It helps us to see our garbage, to acknowledge our darker side, and to recognize that we do, indeed, fail and even sin.

Here's a story from the Talmud: The people of Israel, we are told, find themselves recipients of a particular moment of grace with God and decide to pray for the evil inclination to be handed over to them. And so it is.

They are about to kill off this wickedness when they are warned that doing so would destroy the world. So instead, they imprison the inclination for three days and "looked in the entire Land of Israel for a fresh egg and couldn't find one." So they let the evil inclination go.

The moral: The evil inclination is a necessary part of life. We shouldn't hide from it, tear it apart from our good side, or imprison it. The things that tempt us—ambition, envy, greed—can be channeled for the good if we develop a means of doing so.

There's Growth in the Garbage

So the aim is not to do without the evil inclination and not to disregard it. The aim is to own it. Take responsibility for it. Accept our humanity. And then to tweak it, to use our awareness of our own failings and shortcomings to prod us to understand more deeply the nature of our humanity. From there we know we can be better, we can improve.

That's mindfulness—incorporating both our *schmutz* and our better natures.

Try this visualization exercise: Focus on the image of your mental garbage. As the garbage becomes visible, throw it into heavy-duty, three-ply, industrial-strength plastic garbage bags. Use as many bags as it takes to do the job—you might need only one bag; you might need twenty. As you fill the bags with your mental and emotional garbage, tie them shut with a knot or a twist tie.

It's hard work and it takes practice. But you can't ignore the garbage, the *schmutz*. It won't stay hidden forever.

10

Take a Leap
of Action

Isaac Bashevis Singer used to tell this story. A man, concerned about his wife's fidelity, goes away on a business trip. Before he leaves, he tells his son, "Watch everything your mother does, and give me a complete report when I return."

When the man comes back, he asks his son, "Did Mommy do anything unusual when I was away?"

"The night after you left," the boy says, "a strange man came to the house. He kissed Mommy on the lips when he came in, and they hugged for a long time."

"And then?" the man asks.

"Mommy took him into the bedroom."

"And then?"

"I looked through the keyhole. The man took off all his clothes."

"And then?"

"He started to take off all of Mommy's clothes, and he was kissing her the whole time."

"And then?"

"Then Mommy turned off the lights and I couldn't see anything."

"God in heaven!" declares the man, slapping his cheek. "These doubts will kill me!"[1]

Wrestling with Faith

Some people just can't give up hope, no matter what the evidence suggests. For the Jewish people, it used to be that way about belief in God. Despite the calamities we endured, we believed. Even after Auschwitz, with all our doubts, most of us still believed. But is this still true? Has our belief in God finally been overtaken by our doubts?

One of my bizarre pleasures at my congregation was twice hosting Christopher Hitchens, the late Jewish atheist with an attitude. His book *God Is Not Great: How Religion Poisons Everything* was not only popular in Coral Gables. It spent many weeks at the top of the *New York Times* Best Seller List. Why the huge interest in what an atheist, albeit an articulate atheist, has to say?

I must admit that I have mixed feelings about this phenomenon. On the one hand, I am sorry that people are so critical of God and religion. But on the other hand, I am delighted that so many people are thinking about God and religion, even if their thinking is critical.

As the poet Aaron Zeitlin once wrote, "Praise Me or curse Me, says God.... Cursing is a kind of praise."[2] What we should not do is ignore God.

Let's also understand that this struggle with faith turns out to be a Jewish phenomenon more than a Christian one. Not too long ago a Harris Poll was released showing that, nationwide, just 24 percent of Jews said they were "absolutely certain" there was a God. Maybe in this postmodern world, 24 percent isn't too bad.[3]

But let's view this percentage in a larger context. The same poll found that 76 percent of Protestants and 64 percent of Catholics were certain of God's existence. And 93 percent of Protestant Evangelicals believe in God without question. So we should ask: Why don't more Jews believe in God?

One View of God

Permit me to be personal. I am a genuine Reform Jew in my view of God. I do not think that God wrote the Torah. I do not accept many of the depictions of God in the Bible. I don't choose to believe in the kind of God who would order the wholesale destruction of other peoples. I don't believe in a God who so callously rewards and punishes.

Furthermore, if I believed that God did write the Torah, and therefore the commandments were given by a Commander, I would have to follow them and become Orthodox. How could I live with myself otherwise? I am a Reform Jew precisely because I do not believe that God wrote the Torah.

I like to explain this by referring to a popular song from 1919 that reflected a phenomenon after World War I ended. The hit song was "How Are They Going to Keep Them Down on the Farm Once They've Seen Paree?" Those Kansas farm boys could not return home after seeing the dazzling lights of Paris. Likewise, once you no longer believe in the supernatural happenings of the Bible, it is hard to believe in God in the same way. So you must voyage to a lonelier place where there are no sure things.

Fake It!

But even if I don't believe in the traditional view of God, who is depicted in the Bible as controlling all, punishing the wicked, and rewarding the virtuous, that doesn't mean I have no relationship with God. What it means is that I choose to live in a world—and act—as if there is a God, even though I have no proof of that and often less faith than I would like.

Remember the movie *The Recruit,* with Al Pacino and Colin Farrell? It's about a jaded CIA agent (Pacino) and a CIA trainee (Farrell). In the film, Pacino's character tells the story of an archbishop who is meeting the pope. The archbishop leans into the pope's ear and whispers, "Padre, I cannot continue doing this. I no longer believe in God." To which the pope replies, "Fake it." Such advice may seem cynical, but for those of us caught up in doubts about God, I recommend this advice wholeheartedly. Fake it. Live your life as if God cares how we behave.

Think about Mother Teresa. Her crisis of faith never stopped her from performing acts of loving-kindness. She may have been "faking it," but the slums of Calcutta were a much better place thanks to her divinely inspired dedication. Even when she felt that God had abandoned her, she never wavered from what God called her to do.

Faith Means Action

If the notion of faking our faith in God troubles you, let me suggest a more positive way to think about how we act in a world of divine doubt. In the last century, the greatest teacher about this very subject was the late twentieth-century Jewish theologian Rabbi Abraham Joshua Heschel.

For Heschel, ironically since he was known as a philosopher, religion is not about how we think of God. Heschel does not offer proofs for the existence of God or the truth of religion. As he liked to say, "For the believer, proofs are irrelevant; for the nonbeliever, proofs are unconvincing." According to Heschel, instead of pondering God's presence, we should be asking ourselves how to respond to our indebtedness to God.

For Heschel, history is not the story of the human quest for God, but rather, as he titled his philosophical masterpiece, it is *God in search of man*. God is looking for us, waiting for us. God needs us. The God that Heschel discovers is not the cold, rational God of the philosophers, but the God of the Hebrew prophets, a God who feels and knows the pain of human suffering. This is Heschel's God: the God of the universe who is tormented by the suffering of the poor, the hungry, the helpless, and the hopeless.

Our response to God is through our actions. Words must give way to deeds. Only through our deeds can we worship a God whose name cannot be pronounced.

Heschel's approach to God is nothing less than a Copernican switch. Instead of questioning God, God questions us. Remember that the first question in the Bible is not from a human being to God but from God to a human being, namely, "Where are you?" (This is what God asks Adam, after the fruit has been eaten, in Genesis 3:9.)

And this is still the question that God asks us. Throughout his life, Rabbi Heschel responded to this question by concentrating more on action than on writing. Most people know of Heschel not because of his books but because of his marching for civil rights in Selma, Alabama, and other places. When he marched alongside Martin Luther King Jr. he would say that "even his feet were praying."

For Heschel, we might argue, marching was more important than praying. Action was more important than belief. That's not to say that Heschel did not value belief in God. He was truly God-intoxicated. But his emphasis was on how we respond to God, not what we should demand of God. I find this approach very helpful.

You see, for the Jewish people, belief takes a back seat to actions. Try this experiment: Picture a pair of American Jewish parents who, after being out of touch with their child, a young adult, for a long time, get this phone call. The daughter declares, "I don't observe Jewish holidays. I don't keep kosher. I don't give *tzedakah*. I have not married a Jew. I have no relationship to Israel." Then the child thinks to offer this consolation: "But now I believe in God! I love God, and God loves me! I pray to God."

Question: Does this confession of faith bring the parents any comfort? Not in the Jewish families I know!

What's wrong with this picture? It is wrong because loving God means nothing outside of a context of righteous living.

So my message is: Enjoy the worship. Savor the opportunity to reflect. Appreciate the community. By all means pray to God, but worry more about godliness, the person sitting next to you, and the person living on the street.

Live the Answer

We Jews tend to overthink everything. But life is simpler than we imagine. We are called upon to take God seriously, but not literally.

We are called upon to live our lives not by asking God questions but by answering God's questions. Our task is not to find answers to our questions but to live our very lives as *the answer* to the only questions that really matter: Why are we here? How should we show our gratitude for the fact that we are alive?

Listen to how Heschel himself put it, shortly before he passed away:

> This is the meaning of existence: to reconcile liberty with service, the passing with the lasting, to weave the threads of temporality into the fabric of eternity. The deepest wisdom ... [a person] can attain is to know that his [or her] destiny is to aid, to serve.... The aspiration is to obtain; the perfection is to dispense.[4]

So I challenge us to rise above acquiring and to go for dispensing. To remember that redemption comes to our world not with some grand theological revelation but through simple acts of kindness. Forget the leap of faith. Take a leap of action. Fake it. Live as if there is a God. That's what matters.

One of Rabbi Heschel's heroes was the Hasidic master Levi Yitzchak of Berditchev. The story is told that one year, as Yom Kippur was coming to an end, the people were being led in worship by Levi Yitzchak. All of a sudden, the great rebbe stopped and stood frozen. What had happened? The people knew that their great rebbe's soul had traveled to heaven to speak with the Creator of the universe.

Levi Yitzchak found himself before the Creator, and he said, "God, you expect too much of Your people. We suffer and do our best. Please have compassion on us."

God said, "You know, Levi Yitzchak, you have a point. I will be merciful."

Levi Yitzchak realized that he had caught God in a great mood and decided to press his case. "God, why not save the world now? Bring the Messiah."

God seemed opened to the idea. Levi Yitzchak knew he could save the world today, if he had just a few minutes to convince God.

But in the corner of his eye, Levi Yitzchak saw that, back on Earth at the shul, Samuel the grocer had fainted. He needed to eat. Samuel was not a particularly nice man. And he was stubborn. He would only eat when Levi Yitzchak concluded the service. But to do that, Levi Yitzchak's soul would have to return from heaven. He would not be able to convince God to save the world. But if Levi Yitzchak waited, he knew that Samuel would die.

Levi Yitzchak turned around and went back to Earth. Instead of saving the world, he returned to save one human life.

As he was returning, an angelic choir proclaimed, "Rabbi Levi of Berditchev is indeed saving the world."

Let the atheists have their say, as well as the agnostics. Let them have their best sellers. What matters is not what we believe, don't believe, or don't know we believe. What matters is what we do. What we need is not a leap of faith but a leap of action.

11

Ask Less of the Earth

T here is an old clock tower in Prague that tells time backwards. The clock is in Hebrew and it operates counterclockwise. It is a fascinating creation and I used to wear a watch based on it, which I purchased at one of the synagogue gift shops in Prague. Unfortunately, I would forget that the watch worked backwards and I would miss meetings as a result. What strikes me as most poignant about the clock is that we on Earth cannot turn time backwards. What a shame.

It's a Harsh Reality

I do not want to be an alarmist, but as we face the future, we should admit that our problems are real: The Earth is facing ecological disaster. It does not really matter at this point who gets the blame. The only thing that matters is that we confront the harsh reality of our era. Can anyone doubt the growing threat of climate change and looming environmental calamity? Watch Al Gore's movie *An Inconvenient Truth,* or read the book, and you will not sleep well at night. An article in *Harper's* magazine about what the world will be like when oil really becomes scarce will inspire fear for yourself, your children, and your grandchildren. For instance:

The economy will begin an endless contraction, a prelude to the "grid crash." Cars will revert to being a luxury item, isolating the suburban millions from food and goods. Industrial agriculture will wither, addicted as it is to natural gas for fertilizer and to crude oil for flying, shipping, and trucking its produce. International trade will halt, leaving the Wal-Marts empty. In the United States, northern homes will be too expensive to heat and southern homes will roast. Dirty alternatives such as coal and tar sands will act as a bellows to the furnace of global warming. In response to all of this, extreme political movements will form, and the world will devolve into a fight to control the last of the resources. Whom the wars do not kill starvation will. Man, if he survives, will do so in agrarian villages.[1]

It's enough to make you want to flee to New Zealand and live off the grid. What else can we do about it?

It's Not about "Me," It's about "Us"

One of my favorite Hebrew expressions is *taharog Turkey v'tanuach*, which literally means "Go kill a Turk and relax." The context of the remark is czarist Russia, one hundred years ago or so, when a Jewish boy might be conscripted into the czar's army for decades. The boy tells his mom that he is being drafted and will face terrible challenges on the front. The mother, ever an optimist, says, "Go kill a Turkish soldier and then relax." In other words, do what you have to do and try to stay calm. But as we face the serious challenges before us, we should also consider what we have to do.

The simple answer: Take better care of our Earth. Sometimes we forget that we are not only responsible for ourselves. We are all responsible for each other. There is a famous rabbinic story about two men in a rowboat heading toward land. One man suddenly starts to bore a hole in the bottom of the craft. When challenged, he retorts angrily, "This is none of your business. I am boring the hole under my seat!" The Jewish view is that the Earth is a boat, a conveyance on which we are privileged to ride and be carried.[2] Being responsible passengers means that we need to take seriously issues concerning climate change. We need to work for changes in how our entire country uses energy. Working for change in policies is not enough, however. We also need to change our own wasteful ways. To quote Mahatma Gandhi, "Be the change you want to see in the world."

We all need to reduce carbon dioxide emissions. We need to cut back on driving, when possible. We need to use our air conditioners less in Florida and turn down our thermostats more often in Chicago.

When it comes to the looming environmental crisis, if we are honest with ourselves, we will agree that we are part of the problem, not part of the solution. There is an old saying that is found throughout the forests of Portugal:

> *Let no one say*
> *And say it to your shame*
> *That all was beauty here*
> *Until you came.*

One of the things lost in our culture is the notion that we should dedicate ourselves to something larger than ourselves; that we should leave this place, the planet, a little better than when we came. We really should be embarrassed that we are not doing more to preserve our planet.

Truly we need to "grow up" collectively as well as individually, to learn to feel a sense of shame and responsibility for the things we do as a city, a nation, a world. For decades we have wantonly wasted and hideously abused our environment. Ravaged landscapes and a savaged ecosphere testify to our penchant for destruction and decimation. As our ozone holes grow larger, our water supply grows fouler, and our wildlife grows scarcer, it is high time to feel a societal stab of guilt. It is so easy to become insensitive to what we are doing to our environment. Now is the time, before it is too late, to become activists for our world.

The facts are indisputable: The planet is warming and we are the cause of it. But we do have a window of opportunity as long as we realize that we are at the tipping point. There is no time left to lose.

Our Growing Need for More

The heart of our problem with the Earth is that we consume far too much. The biggest strain on the Earth's resources is not the expansion of people but the growing consumption of the Western lifestyle. The ancient Rabbis understood that wasting resources was an affront to God, what they called *bal tashchit,* or literally, "Don't destroy." I would add, in our day, a related question, "How much is enough?" How many rooms to be heated or cooled do our houses really need? How big must our cars be? In general, what is sufficient for us and what is wasteful?

Recently, I decided to cure my personal gasoline habit and am now leasing an all-electric car. We are fortunate to live in an era when creative solutions are offered; if we are willing to find out about them and take a risk, the new can be good for us and for the planet.

In the Talmud (*Ketubot* 8b) the leading sage Rabban Gamliel complained that people were spending too much on funerals (also weddings), so he instituted the simple ritual that is still the tradition today. Perhaps such an approach might be adopted for our common contemporary *b'nei mitzvah* culture of excess.

There is a rabbinic legend that imagines Noah leaving the ark and seeing that the entire world had been destroyed in a flood. He calls out to complain to God for bringing the waters. God responds, "Noah, I gave you eighty years to build the ark, eighty years to warn the people to change their ways, eighty years to save the Earth. And you did nothing. You warned no one. You only cared about yourself and your family. It is a little too late now to complain. Where were you before?"

Act Now

That's the question asked of us: Where were we? But the only question that matters now is this: What will we do to save our planet?

Should we panic? No. But we need to be focused and motivated. Each of us can make a difference. It is not too late. But the time is now. We are not going to build a clock that allows us to turn back time, but we can move forward by living a little more simply than before. Do not ask yourself how simply you can live, for that is unrealistic. Instead, begin by considering how you can downsize some of your material desires. Remember that these desires, when fulfilled, rarely bring the anticipated joy anyway. In short, be happier with what you already have. Your family and your planet will be grateful.

12

· · · · · · · · · · · ·

Hear the Voice
That Matters

H uman nature being what it is, we can choose to hear or not
hear many things. We can ignore the comments of others when
responding will do no good. I know this is difficult to do, but it is a
vital message in the discipline of *tzimtzum*. If you don't believe me,
consider that if not for this practice, the world could have ended fifty
years ago.

A World of Choices

In October 1962, World War III nearly erupted. As you may remember, when the Soviet Union had placed nuclear missiles in Cuba, the
United States threatened to attack if the missiles were not removed.
Indeed, on October 22 of that year, President John F. Kennedy
warned on television that war might be imminent. He also announced
a blockade against Cuba, escalating the tension between the United
States and the Soviet Union.

A few days later, President Kennedy received two separate messages from Nikita Khrushchev, the leader of the USSR. The first
message was a plea to stop the drift to bloodshed. It was an offer of
compromise in order to prevent the catastrophe of thermonuclear

war. If Kennedy would promise not to invade Cuba, the missiles would be removed.

This conciliatory letter was followed by another message from Khrushchev. But unlike the first note, this time there was a hostile challenge that practically forced the president to declare war. According to historians, Kennedy didn't know which message reflected Khrushchev's true sentiments; he couldn't understand how the same man could send the two contradictory letters. He only knew that he had to do something. Fortunately, his brother Robert "Bobby" Kennedy had a brilliant idea: Forget Khrushchev's bellicose second letter and answer the first one. Ignore the hostile threats and respond to the plea for peace. Bobby's instinct proved correct, and a possible nuclear war was averted.

Undoubtedly, President Kennedy knew that the choice was between far more than two contradictory messages; the lives of millions would be affected. He knew that he had to be tough with the Soviet Union but that peace could come only through compromise.

In essence, President Kennedy had to make two choices: He had to decide what Khrushchev wanted, and he had to decide what he wanted.

A similar choice is featured in the *Akedah,* the binding of Isaac (Genesis 22), the famous Torah portion in which Abraham appears to hear two different voices from God. One voice demands that Abraham kill his son. The other voice demands that he spare his son. One voice threatens to destroy the promise that God had made to Abraham: to make Abraham's descendants through Isaac as numerous as the stars in the sky. The other voice pledges to honor the promise.

Although nuclear destruction does not figure in the *Akedah,* the repercussions of Abraham's decision will be cosmic in terms of the Jewish people. One wrong move and the Jewish enterprise will be over before it's barely begun. Like President Kennedy, Abraham must choose which voice to recognize, and he must also decide which voice inside himself to heed.

Despite the happy ending of the *Akedah,* in which Abraham chooses to hear the voice to save his son, Abraham's dilemma does not conclude with Abraham. Thousands of years later, we too must decide which voice of God we will recognize. As members of a community tied to the Torah, we must choose the kind of God we want to believe in. Specifically, do we pray to a God of cruelty or a God of compassion? Do we believe in a God who tests us or in a God who comforts us? Can we do both?

The Two Voices of God

In his book *Jewish Renewal,* Rabbi Michael Lerner, the founder of *Tikkun* magazine, writes that there are two voices of God in the Torah. One voice is the voice of cruelty. It's the voice that tells the Israelites to destroy all their neighbors when they enter the Promised Land. It's the voice that demands that outsiders be persecuted. It's the voice that says, "Show no mercy" to your enemies.

But there's also another voice of God in the Torah. It's a voice that proclaims that all living beings are created in the divine image. It's a voice that commands us to greet the stranger. It's a voice that preaches peace. According to Lerner, both voices are in our Torah not because God is schizophrenic but because the Torah is a human document. Since fallible human beings created the Torah when responding to divine revelation, they often misunderstood what God wanted. They interpreted their own suffering and painful experiences through a divine lens. The history of persecution, beginning with the exile in Egypt, led to texts that all too often reflect human cruelty instead of reflecting the compassion of God.

Lerner suggests that we respond to the voice of compassion, not the voice of cruelty. To be created in the divine image means to acknowledge the God of life and joy and tolerance, not the God of death and punishment and exclusion. Certainly, both voices can be heard through the texts and traditions of the Jewish people; our task is to respond to the right voice, the voice of love, justice, and mercy.

Such a response involves careful listening. It requires us to struggle with the texts we have. It demands that we constantly ask ourselves: Who is speaking here? Is it the God I believe in? Or is it a distortion, refracted through the painful years of persecution?

Is the voice of God who orders Abraham to kill his son the same voice as the God who demands that he spare his son? How can Abraham decide between the two? Rabbi Lerner would tell us that the voice of cruelty reflects Abraham's warped understanding of what God requires of us. The second voice alone represents the genuine divine will. The first voice is an aberration. The second voice is divine.

Rabbi Lerner's argument is appealing because it allows us to choose the God we want to believe in. But it also forces us to reject a fundamental aspect of the God of our ancestors. In addition, it implies that God is made in our image, in our likeness, instead of our being made in the divine image. I fear that such an approach may be more fantasy than theology.

Fortunately, in *For Those Who Can't Believe,* Rabbi Harold Schulweis also addresses the two portraits of God rendered in the Torah. According to Schulweis, both aspects reflect one God. But since the nature of God is complicated, to say the least, the two aspects appear to be different.

Schulweis points out that in the Bible God has two basic names. First, God is called *Elohim,* which traditionally is translated as "God." In the Bible, *Elohim* is associated with nature, justice, and the harsh realities of life. *Elohim* stands for the way things are. *Elohim* underlies the law of gravity. If you let go of an apple, it will drop, because the law works that way. If an earthquake occurs, buildings may be destroyed, because that's how nature operates. Likewise, if you break a moral law, punishment will follow.

The second name of God is *Adonai*—"Lord" or "Eternal One." *Adonai* is traditionally associated with compassion, love, and hope. It stands not for what is, but for what ought to be. *Elohim* prescribes punishment. *Adonai* teaches transformation. *Elohim* creates the world and all its dangers. *Adonai* inspires human beings to overcome the world's dangers. *Elohim* brings an earthquake or a hurricane. *Adonai* brings rescuers who risk their lives to save the victims and give of their possessions to help the victims cope. *Elohim* is about facts. *Adonai* is about faith.

In the story of the binding of Isaac, it's *Elohim* who tells Abraham to kill his son. In effect, Abraham is being told that everything has its price. If you want to believe in God, you have to sacrifice your dearest dreams. Only by surrendering his beloved son can Abraham prove his worthiness. This is what *Elohim* demands.

But it's *Adonai* who tells Abraham not to complete the sacrifice. It's *Adonai* who says to him, "Your faith has transformed you. The sacrifices I require are within. I seek not cruelty but devotion. Not killing but commitment. Raise the boy. Teach him well. Understand that he belongs to Me and you belong to Me, but it's your lives I seek, not your deaths." And so Abraham, listening to *Adonai,* the voice of hope and compassion, spares his son.

Two Faces of God, One Choice

Of course, the choice that Abraham makes is more complicated than we might think. We cannot merely choose the voice of compassion. We cannot exclusively listen to *Adonai* and ignore *Elohim.* Judaism recognizes both voices because both aspects of God reflect reality.

In our world, there is a natural cause and effect. Smoking can lead to lung cancer. Two automobiles can't inhabit the same space at the same time without a consequence. Moral delinquency affects the innocent as well as the guilty.

Yes, the face of *Elohim* does reflect reality. But where would we be without the face of *Adonai,* leading us to hope for a better world? Where would we be without the voice of compassion, inspiring us to care for people who can never repay us? Where would we be without the faith that, somehow, our lives matter, not only for the work we do but for the examples we set? That, after we're gone, our love and kindness will reverberate throughout the world?

The foundational prayer of the Jewish faith is the *Shema,* which includes these words: "Hear, O Israel, *Adonai* is our *Elohim. Adonai* is One." For us, *Adonai* and *Elohim* are not rival Gods, but two faces of the same God, two voices working in harmony. At times, we will recognize one voice over the other, but neither can exist alone. Whether or not the voices of God in our Torah reflect what God actually said or simply our own divided humanity is ultimately irrelevant. Each of us will hear both voices in our own lives. Each of us will see both *Elohim* and *Adonai* at work.

Like President Kennedy half a century ago, and like Abraham thousands of years ago, our task is to consider the situation we are in and decide how we'll respond. When millions of people in our country have no health care, *Elohim* might say: "If people work, they deserve a doctor's care. If they don't, it's their own fault." *Adonai* might say: "We have to take care of the poor and the needy, despite the drain on our society." When illegal immigrants enter our state, *Elohim* might say: "If people are not here legally, then they have no right to our services." *Adonai* might remind us: "Take care of the stranger, for you were strangers in the land of Egypt." When our children are turning to cigarettes because of sophisticated marketing by tobacco companies, *Elohim* might say: "If you smoke tobacco, you may very well get cancer." And *Adonai* might remind us: "It's our task to protect youngsters from being led astray."

In speaking of the two aspects of *Elohim* and *Adonai,* Rabbi Schulweis acknowledges the need for *Elohim.* We need to be reminded of nature's power, the law of consequences, and the omnipotence of our Creator. But we also need the hope and inspiration of *Adonai.* We need the vision of a compassionate society. We need the dream of peace and healing, the repair of the world, and the binding of bruises. We need to know what reality is but also what reality should be.

Unlike Rabbi Lerner, Rabbi Schulweis understands that the so-called divine voice of cruelty reflects not only basic human hatreds, but basic facts of nature and the way of the world. To put it another way, a deviant can be put in therapy, but you can't psychoanalyze a cancer. A tumor may be terminal, but the care by a loved one may be unending.

So we pray and we listen, straining to hear the voices of God in our daily lives, trying to discern the message so distant and yet so real. A message of truth and transformation, of fact and faith, of law and love.

Shema Yisrael, Adonai Eloheinu, Adonai Echad. O people Israel: *Adonai* and *Elohim* are One. And they are ours. How shall we hear?

13

Don't Underestimate the Power of Small Kindnesses

O nce there was a certain airplane flight from San Francisco to Los Angeles. Like many flights these days, there was a delay. To make matters worse, after the flight took off, it made an unexpected stop in Sacramento. The flight attendant told the passengers they were permitted to leave the plane for thirty minutes. Everybody left the plane except for a blind man. He patiently sat in his seat, with his guide dog quietly by his feet. He was obviously a regular because the pilot approached him by name and asked him if he would like to get off the airplane to stretch his legs.

The man said no, but then observed that his dog would like to stretch *his* legs. Now picture this: All the people in the gate area came to a completely quiet standstill when they looked up and saw the pilot walk off the plane with a guide dog. To make matters worse, the pilot was even wearing sunglasses. People quickly scattered. They not only tried to change planes; they also tried to change airlines!

We Set Our Own Paths

As in this story, sometimes we are misled by what appears to be the truth. We forget that, in life, appearances often are deceiving. Such confusion is found in the famous Torah passage where Pharaoh appears to be God's puppet. The pattern is familiar. As each plague threatens, Pharaoh is given the choice to let the Israelites go. Each time we're told that God "hardens" Pharaoh's heart and he refuses.

A casual reading of the portion suggests that Pharaoh is, as it were, "set up." Nevertheless, some commentators throughout the ages point out that the appearance of free will is deceiving. In reality, Pharaoh alone is responsible for his actions. As they observe, during the early plagues, the Bible says that Pharaoh hardened his own heart. Pharaoh's free will becomes limited only after a pattern of stubborn and insensitive behavior develops. As Rabbi Moses Maimonides wrote:

> We may conclude ... that it was not God who forced Pharaoh to do evil to Israel.... [For no] one forces, preordains, or impels one to take one path over another. Of our own free will do we incline to whatever way we wish to take. This is a fundamental principle of Judaism....[1]

So although it appears that God is controlling Pharaoh, the actual meaning of the biblical story is this: Pharaoh makes so many bad choices that eventually his path is evil. Eventually, the momentum of his recalcitrance and hatred carries him along without his needing to choose. Life chooses for him.

The frightening implication of this lesson is that all of us can be denied choices in life after we have made too many wrong choices. Most of us don't decide one day to be evil people. No one is born with a hardened heart. But if we make enough wrong choices in life, our heart will slowly harden. If we cultivate selfishness, arrogance, and insensitivity, or even if we only mildly entertain such practices, we may not even be aware of how far we've moved from the ideals and expectations of our Jewish tradition in particular and our humanity in general.

Consider this example. Best-selling author Dr. Rachel Naomi Remen tells the story of a woman she knew who got cancer. A male psychiatrist, who was the woman's longtime running partner, began avoiding her, even when she called. Finally, the woman beat her cancer back into remission. Shortly afterward, she ran into the psychiatrist and told him how hurt she was that he hadn't returned her calls. "I'm sorry," he said. "I simply did not know the right thing to say." Remen asked the woman what she would have wanted to hear. She smiled sadly and said, "Oh, something like, 'I heard it's been a hard year. How are you doing?' Some simple human thing like that."[2]

The male psychiatrist was not an evil person, but he had allowed his heart to harden. He had let down a friend, and he did it not because he was uncaring but because he didn't understand that even a small act of kindness would make a difference.

It's Okay to Start Small—Just Start

The same thing happens on a community level. People who care about social justice often feel their little acts won't mean anything, so they do nothing. We don't see ourselves as able citizens who can help heal the world. Maybe we compare ourselves to great social activists like Dr. Martin Luther King Jr. and, knowing we'll never measure up, cease to even try. Or maybe we say that when we retire we will start to care more. Perhaps we are waiting for the courage and wisdom of old age. But, in the meantime, our waiting means not enough is being done to heal the world. It also means that our hearts are slowly hardening. This is the price of endless deferral of trying harder to be better human beings. We never change and we never make a difference.

The good news is that just as our hearts can gradually harden, so too can they gradually soften. To be a good person does not mean we wake up and say, "Okay, it's time to be Mother Teresa." If this were necessary, most of us would despair of ever being good people. Fortunately, softening our hearts is also a subtle enterprise. It happens gradually, in the small but significant details of life.

There's a famous saying credited to the Eastern philosopher Lao-Tzu that a journey of a thousand miles begins with one step. When it comes to softening our hearts, the most important thing to do is begin with an act of kindness. The French theologian Philippe Vernier offers the following advice:

> Do not wait for great strength before setting out for immobility will weaken you further. Do not wait to see very clearly before starting: one has to walk toward the light. Have you strength enough to take this first step?... You will be astonished to feel that the effort accomplished, instead of having exhausted your strength, has doubled it—and that you already see more clearly what you have to do next.[3]

In other words, the secret to opening our hearts is simply to begin.

Kindness Is a Discipline

In her book, *Forgiveness and Other Acts of Love,* Stephanie Dowrick provides a list of such acts:

- Pay attention to what people need, not what you think they need.
- Always give the benefit of the doubt.
- Take responsibility for what happens instead of blaming others.
- Be courteous.
- Bring beauty to all tasks.
- Let go of mistakes.
- Give more than is necessary.
- Appreciate your dependence on others; appreciate their dependence on you.
- Don't keep tabs on what you have given or what you are owed.
- Allow others to give to you.

- Receive gracefully.
- Never use power to wound, undermine, or abuse.
- Take an interest in others' interests.
- Refuse to pass on hurtful gossip.
- Praise lavishly.
- Express gratitude.
- Let past hurts slip away.
- Welcome compromise.[4]

I am sure that we could add to this list. The point is that we understand how such actions, performed with discipline, can make all the difference between slipping into hardheartedness or softheartedness. In short, it's a matter of discipline, of practice.

It's been pointed out that rescuers of Jews in Nazi-occupied Europe usually did not wake up one day as overwhelmingly righteous people. Instead, they first responded to the need of a friend. Only later did they go on to help strangers. Likewise, people today become better people one act of kindness at a time. Children who help teach younger children, who write letters to people in hospitals, or who donate money to buy toys for poor children will be more receptive to helping people as adults. This is because humane morality is like playing the piano. With practice, you get better.

A Hard Heart or a Soft Heart—It's Your Choice

It's also true that such behavior not only softens our own hearts. It can also soften the hearts of others. Consider this story. Baseball legend George Herman "Babe" Ruth was playing one of his last full major league games. The Boston Braves were playing the Reds in Cincinnati. The old veteran wasn't the player he had once been. The ball looked awkward in his aging hands. He wasn't throwing well. In one inning, his misplays allowed most of the runs scored by Cincinnati.

As Babe Ruth walked off the field after making a third out, head bent in embarrassment, a crescendo of "boos" followed him to the dugout. A little boy in the stands couldn't tolerate it. He loved Babe Ruth, no matter what. With tears streaming down his face, the boy jumped over the railing and threw his arms around the knees of his hero. Babe Ruth picked up the boy, hugged him, set him back on the ground, and gently patted his head.

The rude booing ceased. A hush fell over the park. The crowd was touched by the child's demonstration of love and concern for the feelings of another human being.

As this story reminds us, caring is a gift of God that can melt the hardest of hearts. The more we care, and the more others learn to care, the closer we'll come to ushering in an age of peace and blessing for the whole world.

What is most important is for us to recognize how each little action, how each little choice, will move us toward either good or evil. There is no such thing as standing still. Either our hearts will harden or they will soften. By taking on the small challenges of daily life and doing the right thing, we will prepare ourselves for the greater challenges, and we will be making a better world.

The prophet Isaiah addresses people whose hearts have become hardened. Like Pharaoh in the Torah, these people have gradually ceased to care about other people. Through their choices they have become insensitive. They have slowly lost their humanity. The prophet prays that soon they will learn once again to hear with their ears, see with their eyes, and understand with their minds. He hopes that they will hear the cries for help of their unfortunate brothers and sisters, that they will see the poverty and injustice all around them, and that they will understand how each of them can make a difference. The secret is to take the first step.

Then, concludes the prophet, the people will return to God, and they shall be healed. One step—and one day—at a time. That's all it takes.

14

See the Divinity in Others

A few years ago, United Airlines had a terrible day in Chicago. A terminal had to shut down, eighty-one flights were canceled, and six thousand passengers were searched—all because one passenger ran past a security checkpoint and disappeared into the crowd at O'Hare International Airport. The man, carrying a canvas bag, was probably not a terrorist. He probably didn't have a gun or a bomb in his carry-on. He simply didn't have the time to bother with security. So he rushed to his airplane without caring about how his actions might affect others. We should note that this isn't the first time a selfish passenger has ruined the travel plans of thousands of people. A similar incident, affecting seven thousand passengers and forty flights, occurred several years back in Houston.

Unfortunately, such behavior is only an extreme example of a growing trend in our country: rude, uncivil attitudes. The world in which we live is suffering from more and more vulgar speech, indecent behavior, and selfish living. We see it in our entertainment, on our streets, and in the newspaper accounts of hate crimes and vandalism.

Where Did It Go?

It's not that we Americans don't have a lot to celebrate. We can be proud of our many technological accomplishments. We have more resources at our disposal than ever before. Computers and cell phones allow us to conduct our business with great efficiency. Yet such accomplishments have not made us any more civil toward each other as a country. Indeed, in recent years our incivility has only increased.

A perfect example is the cell phone. Witness the behavior of people with cell phones these days. It is no rare thing for a dinner companion to wait fifteen minutes while the other chats on the phone. Important business meetings are put on hold because someone whips out a phone the second it starts ringing. And consider how cell phone use makes bad drivers even worse!

I recently read about a Colorado funeral director complaining about impatient drivers who dart in and out of funeral processions instead of waiting for them to pass. There was a time when, if nothing else, a funeral procession received a little respect. But that time is over. Uncivil drivers are not only rude, they bear a great responsibility for the fact that cars kill far more people each year in our country than handguns do. One of the best bumper stickers I have seen lately declares the following: "Forget about World Peace ... Visualize Using Your Turn Signal!"

These days, things aren't much better up in the sky. Airlines have seen a steady rise in hostile passengers. There was the angry man who threw his suitcase at an airline employee who was eight months' pregnant, all because he missed a connection. Or consider the woman who punched a flight attendant because there were no more sandwiches. It's also true that airline employees themselves have become far less polite in recent years.

There is also a growing incivility in Washington, a phenomenon that will surprise none of us. Concerning this problem, Rabbi David Saperstein, the director of the Religious Action Center of the Reform Movement, declared:

Today the nasty rhetoric and mean-spirited personal attacks that are coming to characterize more and more political campaigns have begun to seep into and poison political debate in Congress, in the media, and in public life generally.[1]

He quoted the talmudic admonition of two thousand years ago that "a person who publicly shames another is like someone who has shed blood."

The growing incivility naturally has trickled down to our children. According to one survey, almost 90 percent of grade-school teachers and principals report that they often face abusive language from students. We have seen the rise of violence in our schools. Guns are readily available and tempers flare easily. As a result, we see school shootings at Columbine High School and Virginia Tech, domestic terrorist attacks committed by children and young adults in schools.

A cover story of an issue of *USA Today* was titled "Excuse Me, But ... Whatever Happened to Manners?" As the article observed, it's getting hard not to notice the "growing rudeness, even harshness, of American life.... An overwhelming majority of Americans—89 percent in one survey—think incivility is a serious problem. More than three in four said it's gotten worse in the past ten years."[2]

My guess is that most of us would agree.

The Paradoxes of Our Time

Why have we become so uncivil? Part of the problem is reflected in the complexity of our age. We have more of what we want than ever before but less ability to enjoy it or to enjoy each other. This complexity is revealed in the following paradoxes of our time:

> *We have taller buildings, but shorter tempers;*
> *wider freeways, but narrower viewpoints;*
> *we spend more, but have less;*
> *we buy more, but enjoy it less.*
> *we have bigger houses and smaller families;*

more conveniences, but less time;
we have more degrees, but less sense;
more knowledge, but less judgment;
more experts, but more problems;
more medicine, but less wellness.
We drink too much, smoke too much, spend too recklessly,
laugh too little, drive too fast, get angry too quickly,
stay up too late, get up too tired, read too little,
watch TV too much, and pray too seldom.
We have multiplied our possessions, but reduced our values.
We talk too much, love too seldom and lie too often.
We've learned how to make a living, but not a life;
We've added years to life, not life to years.
We've been all the way to the moon and back, but have
    trouble crossing the street to meet the new neighbor.
We've conquered outer space, but not inner space;
we've done larger things, but not better things;
we've cleaned up the air, but polluted the soul;
we've split the atom, but not our prejudice.
We write more, but learn less;
plan more, but accomplish less;
we've learned to rush, but not to wait;
we have higher incomes, but lower morals;
more food but less appeasement;
more acquaintances, but fewer friends;
more effort but less success.
We build more computers to hold more information, pro-
    duce more copies than ever, but have less communication;
we've become long on quantity, but short on quality.
These are the times of fast foods and slow digestion; tall men,
    and short character; steep profits, and shallow relationships.
These are the times of world peace, but domestic warfare; more
    leisure, but less fun; more kinds of food, but less nutrition.

*These are the days of two incomes, but more divorce; of fan-
cier houses, but broken homes.*

*These are the days of quick trips, disposable diapers, throw-
away morality, one-night stands, overweight bodies, and
pills that do everything from cheer to quiet to kill.*

*It is a time when there is much in the show window and
nothing in the stockroom.*[3]

As these paradoxes show us, contemporary life has many pressures,
despite the prosperity. Unfortunately, an early casualty of such pressures is the civility we sorely lack.

The Glue That Binds Us

It's important to point out that when I use the term *civility* I mean far
more than good manners. Manners are cultural and therefore relative.
Good manners in Miami may be somewhat different than good manners in Manhattan. *Civility* is a broader, more absolute term. Stephen
Carter, a professor of law at Yale University, defines *civility* as "the
sum of the many sacrifices we are called to make for the sake of living
together."[4] I like this definition because it reminds us that the goal of
civility is not to know which knife to use with our butter. The goal
is to get along together. The only way to reach this goal is through
sacrifice. It can only be achieved by giving people the respect they
may not deserve but is ours to bestow anyway. Such people may not
have earned our civility, but we are civil not because the world is fair
or because being civil gives us pleasure. We are civil because, in the
end, it is only such respectful behavior that binds us together as a community. Without such behavior, we have nothing to hold us together.

In Judaism we have a Hebrew expression for this kind of civility:
derech eretz. Literally meaning "the way of the land," the term refers
to common decency and civility. Our heritage even proclaims that
the Torah itself means nothing if people don't practice *derech eretz,*
if people aren't willing to make the sacrifices needed to live together.

I would like to imagine what a more civil world might be like, to consider what we should be doing to make such civility a greater part of who we are and what we do. I would like us to see how *derech eretz* might help us refine our society and give us more hope for a future of kindness and understanding, instead of the mean and cold climate too prevalent on our streets and in our world today.

Hello, Fellow Passenger

When it comes to civility, we should first understand that genuine civility requires us to make sacrifices, even for strangers. The essence of civility is giving up something for the sake of someone else. In some contexts, this logic of self-sacrifice is easy to grasp. For instance, in the nineteenth century, as railroad travel became commonplace, there were so many people crammed into tight spaces that people needed to sacrifice some of their independence for the common good. To help such people practice civility, Isaac Peebles wrote a best seller titled *Politeness on Railroads*. Here was some of the advice:

> [W]hispering, loud talking, immoderate laughing, and singing should not be indulged by any passenger. Passengers should not gaze at one another in an embarrassing way. [In addition, conductors cracked down on passengers who] indulg[ed] personal preferences at the expense of other passengers.[5]

Unfortunately, in the twenty-first century, we travel under the illusion that we are no longer sharing tight spaces and therefore such sacrifices are no longer necessary. As it's been pointed out, we care less and less about our fellow citizens, because we no longer see them as our fellow passengers.

To put it another way, when we travel on a train together, it's easy to remember that we are sharing a journey. When people are driving alone in their cars, facing traffic from the other direction, it's harder to recognize that shared journey. However, like travelers in a fourth-class railway car, the journey will be impossible if we aren't prepared to make sacrifices for the comfort of others.

Our society will continue to decline if we are unable to make personal sacrifices for the greater good. We need to be better at tolerating the poor driver who makes us late; we need to keep our mouths closed when some foolish person's banter invites a stinging comeback; we need to become less self-absorbed and more aware of the people around us. We need to remember their needs and feelings, not only because it will make us feel better in the end. It is simply the right thing to do. It is *derech eretz*.

Civility Allows for Respectful Criticism

Of course, the willingness to make sacrifices does not mean there won't be occasions when we will need to criticize others. Silent tolerance is not always the right response. American humorist and writer Oliver Herford may have had this in mind when he observed that "a gentleman is one who never hurts anyone's feelings unintentionally." That is, there will be times when we need to confront another human being. Nevertheless, we should understand that our criticism should always be done in a civil manner. Any genuine civility must allow us to criticize others but not by jettisoning the respect we owe all God's creatures.

In the Talmud (*Arachim* 16b), we find a famous debate between the Rabbis concerning how one should rebuke another. All of them agree, however, that when confronted with people behaving unjustly, we are obligated to criticize them. The issue centers not on *if* we should rebuke them but on *how* we should rebuke them. Rebuking someone may be necessary, but shaming them in public never is. In addressing a minor wrong by publicly castigating the offender, we end up committing a major one. Therefore, the decision to criticize, as well as how to do it, should be considered very carefully.

When it comes to deciding whether or not to criticize someone, Rabbi Joseph Telushkin provides the following advice. First, we should ask ourselves how offering the criticism makes us feel. Does it give us pleasure or pain? If a part of us relishes the idea of rebuking the person, we probably shouldn't do it. But if we truly don't want to make the criticism and yet feel morally obligated to do so, then chances are we are doing the right thing.

Our criticism should also be nonthreatening and useful to the one being criticized. The medieval Jewish philosopher Moses Maimonides puts it like this: "He who rebukes another ... should administer the rebuke in private, speak to the offender gently and tenderly, and point out that he is only speaking for the wrongdoer's own good...."[6] I personally have found that when admonishing someone, it's important to avoid judgmental words like *bad* or *unprofessional,* which immediately put the person being criticized on the defensive.

Aim for Royal Respect

In general, criticism should never be used to push people down while raising us up. Critical words should never be said in haste or without humanity. Never should our goal be to make the other person feel bad. Think about how much more civil life would be if we remembered to always care about the person whom we are addressing.

Indeed, when it comes to civility, the sacrifices we make and the sensitivity we observe all boil down to one golden rule: Remember the divinity in each other. This is our greatest challenge and our greatest hope. In an age of increasing violence in our entertainment and everyday speech, not to mention the vicious personal attacks in politics, civility means restoring a sense of awe for all human beings. This approach is reflected in a common synonym for *civility,* the word *courtesy.* This word actually comes from the word *court.* As the name implies, when it comes to courtesy, we are supposed to treat others like royalty. We are supposed to be as considerate of others as if they were genuine nobility. Imagine how much more civility we would have if we treated one another in this way. Not only would our own behavior improve, but we might even improve the behavior of others.

This lesson is reflected in the stage version of *The Man of La Mancha,* the story of Don Quixote. The play features a waitress and prostitute named Aldonza. When Don Quixote sees her, he refuses to treat her as a prostitute. Instead, he calls her "my Lady." He actually gives her a new name, Dulcinea. Even after she is raped, and Don Quixote finds her hysterical and disheveled, he says compassionately, "My Lady, Dulcinea, oh my Lady, my Lady."

> "Don't call me a lady," she cries. "O God, don't call me a lady. Can't you see me for what I am? I was born in a ditch by a mother who left me there naked and cold—too hungry to cry.... Don't call me a lady. I'm only Aldonza. I'm nothing at all."

As she runs into the night, Don Quixote calls out, "But you are my Lady."

At the end of the play, the Man of La Mancha is dying alone, despised and rejected. To his deathbed comes a Spanish queen with a mantilla of lace. Quietly she kneels beside him and prays. He opens his weak eyes and says, "Who are you?"

"My Lord, don't you remember? You gave me a new name; you called me Dulcinea. I am your Lady."

Don Quixote refused to treat Aldonza with anything less than royal respect. And so this is what she became. Likewise, if we treat others with civility and courtesy—as noble people, as people with souls—just maybe we are helping them to grow into civil and courteous people. In doing so, we'll be making a more humane society for us all.

It Comes Down to Divinity

This is not always easy, of course. If a man cuts me off in traffic, I can certainly think of a more gratifying response than pleasantly waving to him. It's also more gratifying to yell at an incompetent salesperson than to patiently smile at her. But when we act with civility, contrary to our instincts, we are giving ourselves a gift. For although in the short term showing our anger may feel wonderful, down the road we will most likely feel bad for behaving that way, and we will have contributed to the growing incivility around us.

To help us be more civil, and therefore observe the mitzvah of *derech eretz,* I recommend keeping at the forefront of our minds the declaration of the great sage Ben Azzai. "The most important teaching in the Torah," he observed, "is that God created us as one human family" (Jerusalem Talmud, *Nedarim* 9:4, 41c). To which we can add that we are endowed with a measure of God's spirit as well. Everything we do and every attitude we possess depend on whether or not we believe these crucial words. They tell us that each of us, as human beings, deserves some basic dignity because of the divine spark inside us. These words tell us that to be cruel to others, even in some small way, is to be cruel to God.

A final story may help us in confronting the challenge of civility: In an event at the Special Olympics, nine athletes with physical and/or mental disabilities were competing in the hundred-yard dash. During the race, one boy fell down and began to cry. When they heard the crying, the other eight runners slowed down and paused. Each one in turn went back to the fallen boy. One girl with Down syndrome bent down, kissed him, and said, "This will make you better. This will make you better." Then all nine linked arms and walked together to the finish line.

Would that we learned the lesson of these nine special athletes. The point of our lives is not to win the race, to step on others, or to rejoice in their downfall. We're here together on a journey that will only succeed when we realize that we are all fellow travelers, all possessing a divine soul, and all on a path toward redemption. To be civil means to make sacrifices, to share our honest feelings but never with malice, and to see the good in every person. It's to recognize our fellow human beings for who they really are: children of God in need of our kisses and hugs, in need of our assurances and love.

Civility means holding ourselves back, because in the holding back we make room for what matters most.

15

Recognize There Are No Guarantees

On the morning of June 24, 1993, David Gelernter, a professor of computer science at Yale University, opened a package he'd received in the mail. Suddenly it blew up and nearly killed him. Gelernter was the twenty-third victim of the Unabomber, the man now identified as Theodore Kaczynski. As with his other victims, Gelernter had never even met Kaczynski.

Bleeding profusely, Gelernter managed to drag himself to the university clinic. When he arrived, his blood pressure was nearly zero. The bomb had blasted away much of Gelernter's right hand and shattered the wrist, broken his left hand, inflicted deep wounds on his chest and right leg, and permanently damaged his right eye so that his vision on that side is constantly blurred. He endured months of reconstructive surgery, but nevertheless, because of the bomb he will carry severe scars on his body for the rest of his life.

As it happens, David Gelernter is an observant Jew. He grew up on the Bible stories that recount how God delivered those faithful ones who suffered. He learned that faith is not the absence of doubt, but the presence of courage. Drawing on this perspective, he wrote:

So: What's the scoop on surviving a mail bomb? What do you learn? You learn that, at first, the past will seem only like a cause for mourning, but your job is to twist it around and make it a cause to rejoice. At the end of meals every Sabbath, observant Jews sing a psalm: "Those that sow in tears will reap shouting with joy. Weeping as he goes, he carries the seed bag—and returns with shouts of joy...." [In other words, if] ... you focus the big sweep of history on a single lifetime, the [Psalmist] says, you see life as a stubborn return from sorrow again and again.[1]

For most of us, David Gelernter's courageous attitude is not only inspirational. It's practically unbelievable. To give lip service to the power of faith to turn our mourning into joy is not unusual. Yet to live through a nightmare and respond with joy and gratitude is no small feat. Given the same awful circumstance, would we respond with such faith? I hope we will not have to find out. But this I know: In the face of actual tragedy, the ability to shout with joy seems unimaginable.

The Ups and Downs of Faith

As an observant Jew, David Gelernter may have a more active faith from which to draw support, and yet even Orthodox Jews surely must have their doubts at times about God and God's role in our life. To be human means to live with, at best, a "moody faith." Moments of confidence and joy in the gifts of life will be tempered with times of terrible questioning and anxiety. No one is immune from such highs and lows, from such periods of answers and questions. As the poet Robert Browning once observed, an irreligious person is one who lives a life of doubt diversified by faith, while a pious person is one who lives a life of faith diversified by doubt.

Most of us would not identify ourselves at either pole of intense skepticism or boundless faith. We fall into the vast middle ground of wanting to believe but finding ourselves challenged by a harsh reality of injustice and sadness. We want to believe in a Higher Power. We want the universe to make sense. We seek consolation in the teachings of our tradition. But we also have our doubts, and these doubts are usually produced by our disappointments. If everything went well in our lives, if our expectations were always met, if we suffered no personal loss, who among us would have doubts about God and the goodness of life?

The Weight of Unspoken Promises

We know, of course, that no one alive is free of such suffering and disappointment. It is part and parcel of the human condition. Most of us recognize this sad truth and have even come to terms with a tolerable level of sadness. Yet there are still certain disappointments that challenge the very foundations of our life. I speak not only of great personal tragedies, such as the loss of a child. I also refer to relatively small setbacks that lead us to question everything we hold dear in life. The underlying principle of such disappointments is that they are completely unexpected. They are things that we never thought we would have to worry about.

We might call these "unspoken promises." These are the goals and enjoyments in life we assume are ours to expect, almost as a right of being alive. In our expectations we are like the Israelite farmer described by the prophet Isaiah. The farmer carefully planted his vines, built a watchtower for fortification, and had a winepress hewn out of stone. Then he waited for good grapes, but wild grapes grew instead. So the farmer cries out, "What else can I do to my vineyard that I did not do? Why did I hope for good grapes but receive wild ones?" He had done everything right, but the loss still was his to bear. The unspoken promise that his hard work would be rewarded was not fulfilled.

Thousands of years later, we have our own unspoken promises. Perhaps they involve our children. Some children are labeled as "promising." What this usually means is that they possess certain abilities and talents, and their parents invest in them the love and care and instruction necessary to nurture these talents. But there is no guarantee that such children will live up to their side of the bargain. Nor is it clear that they ever agreed to the arrangement in the first place. After all, there was no verbal or written contract offered. Of course, try explaining that to the disappointed parent. Such parents have gazed at their tiny baby in a crib and felt all their hopes for the future embodied in that bundle. Who can deny them their dreams?

The same disappointment takes place in reverse, when children grow up and realize that their parents never fulfilled their unspoken promise to nurture their children by providing a safe and sacred home. They realize that they were cheated out of an agreement never stated but nonetheless real.

Unspoken promises also find their way into our general attitudes about life. Every time we feel that life should be fair, we are reflecting an unspoken promise. Every time we think we should be rewarded for being good, or expect that life will have a happy ending if we try our best, we are being just like the Israelite farmer. Whenever we do everything right and expect happiness in return, we are hoping the world will keep its unspoken promise to us.

No More Pretending

Such beliefs will never lead to happiness or even contentment of any kind. Instead, we must surrender such expectations if we want to find peace of mind. This begins with considering anew the unspoken promises that fill our lives and that may lead to bitterness and disappointment. We should ask ourselves: What unspoken promises are we counting on to come true? And how will we respond to life if they should not be fulfilled? Will our disappointment lead to doubt, or can we turn our loss into a richer life, filled with renewed faith? Can we accept that life gives us no guarantees and still find joy in our days? Can we turn our suffering into serenity?

When it comes to unspoken promises, the first thing to do is to bring them to the surface, to make the hidden revealed. In order to be aware of our unspoken promises, we need to confront some painful possibilities that we would rather ignore. As Ralph Waldo Emerson once observed, "Life invests itself with inevitable conditions, which the unwise seek to dodge." We would like to be exempt from these inevitable conditions or at least pretend that they won't happen for a very long time. We may also accept these conditions intellectually, but accepting them emotionally is another matter entirely.

Psychotherapist Robert Gerzon has compiled a list of such conditions, which he calls "The Least Favorite Laws of Life." Let's see how many of our unspoken promises would be challenged by these cold splashes of reality:

Life is suffering.

God loves us, but that does not entitle us to special treatment because God loves everyone else just as much.

Life does not come with any guarantees.

Our bodies can malfunction and are subject to injury and illness.

Bad things happen to good people.

There are no magic potions, no panaceas.

Not everyone we meet will like us.

The more we genuinely love and care about other human beings, the more anxiety we experience concerning their well-being.

Every advantage is accompanied by a disadvantage.

The disasters that actually befall us in life are often ones we never even considered.

Money, even lots of money, can only buy things that can be bought.

Sometimes our worst fears do come true.

Everything changes.

Just because we love someone, that does not mean that he or she will love us in return.

Some of our most cherished dreams may not come true, no matter how much we want them to.

The chances are very high that we never got all our important needs met in childhood. Nevertheless, we are completely responsible for who we are today.

Sometimes there are no second chances.

Despite the human relationships we have, we remain separate individuals and face life (and death) alone.

Life is not always fair, at least in the short run of one lifetime.

Evil exists.

We will never be free of problems because every solution inevitably creates a new problem.

Our defenses keep us from experiencing love and peace.

Without our defenses we would feel absolutely terrified.

Because we inevitably hurt and are hurt by one another, we need to forgive ourselves and each other endlessly.

We are really going to die.

Our time of death is unknown; it may occur today.

Our manner of death is unknown; it may be painful.

Because life involves anxiety, pain, and suffering, we desperately need each other's love and acceptance.

[And finally, the] ... Least Favorite Laws of Life apply to all of us.[2]

This list, which is by no means exhaustive, should make us reconsider (or recognize for the very first time) the unspoken promises underlying in our lives. If any of these least favorite laws of life challenge any presumptions we have held about how life will treat us, then we have set ourselves up for disappointment.

If we expect that any of these laws do not apply to us, we will be like the sixty-something woman who told me that, after losing her ninety-year-old father, she did not believe in God anymore. Although I understood her pain in losing her loved one, at the time her declaration of doubt made no sense to me. How could anyone not believe in God after losing a parent who had reached the fullness of years? Now I understand that her disappointment was more than grief over losing a beloved parent. An unspoken promise—that her father would always be there for her—had been broken. So she couldn't believe in God anymore. Or more precisely, she couldn't believe in a God who had promised that her father would live forever.

Life Promises Us Nothing

My message to this grieving woman, and to all of us, is to suggest that such unspoken promises lead us down the wrong path in life. To believe in such promises is to set the stage for toxic anger and resentment. Surely there must be another way.

Such a way would be to admit that that our unspoken promises are not valid and binding. Indeed, perhaps this is the true message of the holiest declaration in Judaism on the holiest night of the year, *Kol Nidrei*: Life does not promise us anything. Life comes with no guarantees. The Midrash (ancient stories and biblical commentary by the sages) teaches us this lesson in a story of a rabbi who attends the *brit* of the son of a friend. At the celebration, the father of the boy invites all the guests to return many years later for his son's wedding. The rabbi then departs, despite the late hour, and begins walking home. The angel of death meets him on the road, and the rabbi, unaware of the angel's identity, notices that the angel looks upset.

"Forgive me for asking," he says, "but you look very troubled. What is bothering you so much?"

The angel responds, "I am the angel of death, and I am so tired of people who take their blessings for granted. The man who celebrated his son's *brit* today invited everyone to attend the wedding, and yet his son will not live thirty days more."

The story ends with the rabbi anxiously inquiring if the angel has "official business" with him, and the angel responds by saying, "Don't worry, Rabbi, it's not your time, but just the same, you shouldn't go out on these roads late at night."[3]

Beyond this piece of good advice, the angel reminds all of us that we simply cannot know what tomorrow will bring and so therefore we must understand how precious each day is. For unspoken promises of tomorrow may very well be broken.

Obviously, for parents the death of a child reflects the most severe broken promise imaginable. But even the path of life that healthy children choose to take can be a source of profound disappointment to their parents.

Most parents try their hardest to raise children who will make them proud and return their love. But there is no guarantee. When the promising child disappoints, all we are left with is the question poignantly asked by politician and presidential hopeful George McGovern, after his daughter died of an overdose: "What could I have done differently?" Often the terrible, frustrating answer is this: Nothing. These things just happen. They are broken, unspoken promises—and they will continue to be broken. We can either be consumed by feelings of guilt and depression or we can accept the fact that life carries no guarantees.

Succumbing to Sacred Suffering

Here's an example from a colleague of mine, author and theologian Rabbi Bradley Shavit Artson, and his son, Jacob. As Jacob became a toddler, Rabbi Artson and his wife began noticing that Jacob's development wasn't normal. Eventually, they discovered that he was autistic. When he learned about his son's condition, Rabbi Artson noted, "I felt as though the entire universe had caved in, that we were the living dead. I had been betrayed by God, and the cosmos, and by everything." As time went on, the disappointment in his son's illness did not disappear, but joining it was a new insight into life.

> Jacob has taught me to let go of the future. Jacob has taught me all the thousands of expectations and impositions that I didn't even know I had and that I had to give up. And I discovered them only when I realized I couldn't have them anymore. We tell ourselves, "Oh, our children can grow up to be anything, they can grow up to do anything, they can have whatever life they want to have," and it's nonsense. We don't even know the extent of what we demand of them until they won't do it. And then suddenly we realize how very much we want for them and from them.[4]

As Rabbi Artson points out, we only realize what we have lost when it is gone. Such a realization means all of us should be more aware of the gifts we enjoy, even as we surrender our belief that such gifts cannot be taken away. Even as we say good-bye to the dreams we have for ourselves and our families that won't come true. Our disappointments will be real, but they can be placed into a sacred context of not taking anything or anyone for granted.

In such a sacred context, we can learn that the love we have for others doesn't stop just because our unspoken promises may be broken. Although life comes with no guarantees, this does not keep us from trying to give as much as we can to those we love and the world around us. We should never let the possibility of future pain preclude us from present joy.

In 1968, college student Kent Keith succinctly summed up what this means:

If people are unreasonable, illogical, and self-centered—love them anyway.

If you do good, people will accuse you of selfish, ulterior motives. Do good anyway.

If you are successful, you win false friends and true enemies. Succeed anyway.

The good you do today will be forgotten tomorrow. Do good anyway.

Honesty and frankness make you vulnerable. Be honest and frank anyway.

People favor underdogs, but seem to follow only top dogs. Fight for underdogs anyway.

What you spend years building may be destroyed overnight. Build anyway.

People really need help, but may attack you if you help them. Help people anyway.

Give the world the best you have and you may get kicked in the teeth. Give the world the best you've got anyway.[5]

To which I would add: There are no guarantees in this life that our kindness and love will be rewarded, but we should love and care for each other anyway.

16

Let Go of Fear
by Facing It First

Try as we might, many of us are not very good when it comes to flying in airplanes. We know the odds are overwhelmingly on our side, but we still get frightened. For those of us who fear flying, these lines, supposedly overheard on actual flights, may not do much to ease our fears:

- There may be fifty ways to leave your lover, but there are only four ways out of this airplane.

- Your seat cushions can be used for flotation, and in the event of an emergency water landing, please take them with our compliments.

- Should the cabin lose pressure, oxygen masks will drop from the overhead area. Please place the bag over your own mouth and nose before assisting children or adults acting like children.

- To operate your seat belt, insert the metal tab into the buckle and pull tight. It works just like every other seat belt, and if you don't know how to operate one, you probably shouldn't be out in public unsupervised.

- In the event of a sudden loss of cabin pressure, oxygen masks will descend from the ceiling. Stop screaming, grab the mask, and pull it over your face. If you have a small child traveling with you, secure your mask before assisting with theirs. If you are traveling with two small children, decide now which one you love more.

An airline pilot tells us that on a particular flight, he had hammered his ship into the runway really hard. The airline had a policy that required the pilot to stand at the door while the passengers exited, giving them a smile and a "Thanks for flying XYZ airline." He said that, in light of his bad landing, he had a hard time looking the passengers in the eye, thinking that someone would have a smart comment. Finally, everyone had gotten off except for a little old lady walking with a cane. She said, "Sonny, mind if I ask you a question?"

"Why no, ma'am," said the pilot. "What is it?"

The little old lady said, "Did we land or were we shot down?"

Fear—The Good and Bad of It

I suppose it's good when we can laugh at our fears, although this is not always easy to do. It is especially sad when fear keeps us from enjoying life as much as we might. Those who fear flying may choose not to travel, missing wonderful opportunities to see friends and family or to explore the world. Even if they go, they may be too anxious to enjoy the journey.

Of course, there are many other things to fear besides airplanes. We may fear crime, disease, or the ending of a relationship. As teenagers, probably the most feared four words in the English language would come from the boy or girl on whom we had a terrible crush. Decades later these words still terrify: *Let's just be friends.*

There is nothing wrong with fear, to some extent. A little fear keeps us from recklessly endangering our lives. It stops us from engaging in the fad titled BASE jumping. *BASE* stands for buildings, antennas, spans, and Earth, and refers to not-so-high places from which people parachute. These places are high enough for the jump to kill us but barely high enough for the parachute to open. Many people die engaging in such activities. Fear that keeps us from such stupidity is reasonable fear.

The lesson is not that we should never fear anything. The problem is that many of us fear too many things too much of the time. Mark Twain used to say that he feared many terrible things in his life, very few of which actually happened to him.

How can we tell when our fears are neurotic and when they are justified? This is a question I often ponder. When we are faced with a true "God forbid" scenario, how should we respond? Can our Jewish faith help us? Can we find comfort in our community? Or is our modern, rational Jewish perspective no match for the demons of despair and anxiety?

Rachel Naomi Remen is a doctor and counselor to people with cancer. In her book *My Grandfather's Blessings,* Dr. Remen tells of the time a woman in her thirties approached her at a party. She told the author a tragic story. Her husband had died young of cancer three years before, and she still could not think of it without anger. As each therapy failed, he had become increasingly withdrawn and rejecting, lashing out at everyone and refusing to let anyone comfort him. Eventually, he died alone, with only the family he had abused at his side. Upon hearing this sad story, Remen asked the woman what she had learned about death from this terrible experience. She paused for a moment and then with great passion she said, "I do not want to die this way." In response, Remen asked her a simple yet profound question: "So how do you need to live? How do you need to live to be sure that you do not die this way?"

To put the question another way, how might we choose to live so that, even when life throws us terrible curves, we can still find meaning in life? I believe that how we respond to our fear is a spiritual issue. And I believe there is wisdom out there to help us face our fears.

Conquering Fear Begins with Acknowledging It

When it comes to fear, the first lesson is that we must learn to face our fears, not ignore them. In our tradition, courage is an important value. From a spiritual perspective, we don't handle fear by shunting it aside. We don't simply try to whistle a happy tune and drive our fears away. Instead, we face our fears.

On the surface, facing our fears doesn't seem logical. If you are afraid of something, and you share your fears with others, they will tend to play down your fear. They will say, "Don't worry. Things will probably be okay." That may be true, but such reassurances often fall flat. You might say, "Thank you," but what you're thinking is, "That's easy for you to say." The truth is that when we are afraid, it's almost impossible to whistle our fears away. We can distract ourselves from them, but they always come back. After all, fear is a feeling, and feelings are like the weather. They come and go of their own accord. So it doesn't help to ignore our fears.

Instead, we must learn to accept them. Consider this advice from physician Dennis Gersten. When trying to alleviate fear in cancer patients, he uses several symptomatic treatments. But the fear is often so enormous that it transcends these techniques. With cancer especially, the initial diagnosis triggers overwhelming fear. Even after people have been treated and the cancer is gone, they often harbor a deep fear of recurrence.

So in the case of overwhelming fear, Dr. Gersten often asks people to simply observe the fear without trying to push it away, to let their minds explore the fear. He says to them:

> Where is the fear in your body? What are the fearful thoughts and images? Just observe ... allowing the fear to arise, change, and dissolve. Let the fear float. Let it break free from the clutches of your mind. Let yourself be fully immersed in the fear. Embrace the fear.[1]

As Dr. Gersten reports, the results are powerful. The experience of embracing the fear, immersing oneself in the fear, transforms the fear. It doesn't go away, but it also does not haunt us in the same way. Even the fear of death is alleviated by using this approach. Whether someone is suffering from intense pain, fear, or any other overwhelming feeling or symptom, embracing fear is a powerful tool.

Embracing fear doesn't seem like the logical response, but fear itself is rarely logical. So when it comes to fear, we need to feel the fear instead of chasing it away.

A few years ago I had a health scare of my own, which turned out to be nothing. But at the time I simply could not chase away my fears. So I just accepted them. Don't get me wrong, I was still a wreck, but at least I was able to let go of the burden of pretending my fears shouldn't be there.

Often I find myself giving this advice to those who are anxious about the future. Yes, I say, be positive. Yes, whatever it is, we will face it together. But I also say, it's okay to be afraid. It's okay to feel fear. Our feelings are smarter than we think. We cannot ignore them, so we must address them.

Putting Fear in Perspective

Of course, it's not enough to face our fears. We must also learn to work through them. Even if we are not confronting an immediate threat, fear may still be a reasonable response to our life circumstances. Let's be honest. The world is scary. People become ill. Criminals are out there. Not every plane is safe, and not every driver sober. At the root of these fears is the fear of loss. Our fear is grounded in the knowledge that we have something or someone to lose. We can lose the job, the family, the house, our money to the robber, or life itself. It's all at stake; in short, there is not a moment when we are totally safe. There is no trouble-free Eden out there. All of us will be required to move on despite our fears.

My friend and colleague Rabbi Sheldon Marder once shared with me this insight: Joseph Heller's novel *Good as Gold* features a conversation between the main character and his doctor. The doctor tells him, "Your cholesterol and uric acid are up, but not dangerously. Your blood nitrogen is high, but I don't worry about that, mainly because it's your blood nitrogen and not mine. The growth on your lung still doesn't show up on the x-ray. Your prostate is slightly enlarged, but so is mine.... In short, you are falling apart rapidly at a healthy, normal rate. How are things at home?"[2]

This is a good conversation for us to consider as we ponder the place of fear in our lives. There is always something we can find to worry about, if we choose to. It doesn't take a tragedy. Life's uncertainty makes it hard for us to not be afraid. Courage may mean nothing less or more than learning to live with the fact that, like the patient in the story, we too are falling apart rapidly at a healthy, normal rate. When you come right down to it, the best question may be: So how are things at home? Ultimately, we are not in control of what the future will bring, but we can strive to appreciate what we currently have, and we can become adept at living without knowing all the answers.

Fear: A Path to Compassion

Also, for those of us prone to worry, we can try to place our fears in perspective. Without ignoring them, we can go about our business. We can do what needs to be done. We can clean the house, shop, go to work, listen to other people's stories, and maybe care a little more about them. "What doesn't kill me, makes me stronger," declared the German philosopher Friedrich Nietzsche, and when it comes to fear, he was right. If our fears don't overwhelm us, they can sensitize us to the pain and suffering of others.

A wonderful example of such an approach is reported by Hamilton Jordan in his book *No Such Thing as a Bad Day*. This is a man who has had plenty to worry about. In addition to a very stressful tenure in Jimmy Carter's White House, he faced three types of cancer before turning fifty. He was diagnosed with non-Hodgkin's lymphoma, melanoma, and prostate cancer. In all three instances, he chose to deal with his anxiety by helping others.

During his first bout with cancer, he quickly learned that there were two basic types of patients. The first type kept to themselves. Their bitterness and resentment were almost palpable. They deliberately cut themselves off from family and friends. The second type had a different attitude and approach to their illness. Jordan called them "happy warriors." They formed a support group for each other.

> Regardless of the disease or prognosis, these patients would bring cookies for the nurses, tell funny stories to other patients, give hugs to those having a difficult time, and sit and hold the hands of those suffering and dying from cancer. The "happy warriors" were enjoying every minute of life in spite of their cancer, were nurturing to and nurtured by others, and were determined to live every day to the fullest. They were marching to the beat of a different drummer ... possibly to Bonnie Raitt, who sings, "Life seems more precious / When there is less of it to waste."[3]

These people felt fear; I am sure of it. But they were able to soldier on in spite of their fear and bring blessings of kindness and love to others who were suffering. They may have been dying themselves, but they were more alive than most people who are healthy. They faced their fears and they lived with them as well as they could. My guess is they also never lost hope.

Finding Hope Amid Fear

This leads us to another wise choice when facing fear. We must never lose hope in the future. As on old saying puts it, "During the time of the darkest night, act as if the morning has already come." Or as

Albert Camus put it, "In the midst of winter I found within me an invincible summer."

Why is hope so important? For one thing, there is a pragmatic value to being hopeful. Studies show that the body, as well as the heart, heals much better with hope, even if we have to fake our optimism in the beginning. As journalist and author Norman Cousins once reported, 649 oncologists were asked what psychological and emotional factors in their patients seemed important to them. Over 90 percent of those surveyed assigned the highest value to the attitudes of hope and optimism.

Beyond its utilitarian value, a hopeful spirit also reflects a vital teaching of our Jewish tradition: We are never alone, even in our suffering and fear. God is always with us, although at times we may feel only God's absence. To put it another way, we may have given up on God, but God does not give up on us. Although in our fear and anxiety we might even lash out at God, cursing God for making us carry such burdens, somehow we know that, despite our anger, God is not angry at us. God is not punishing us. Rather, God is suffering with us and hoping with us. Such faith is not easy, of course, but it can be found. Sometimes it is the only thing we have left, so it has to be enough.

The most dramatic illustration I have ever heard about such faith comes from the dark night of the Holocaust. It's a tale of Gisella Perl. In March 1944, she was seized by the Gestapo, along with her parents, her husband, and her teenage son. She came from Sighet, Elie Weisel's hometown. She was taken to Auschwitz and, being a physician, was put to work under the infamous Dr. Josef Mengele. Mengele performed savage medical experiments on prisoners, especially women and the disabled. He would tell pregnant women to report to him so that he could send them to another camp for better nutrition. Women would run to him and tell him, "I'm pregnant!" Dr. Perl soon discovered that these women were then taken to the research block and used as guinea pigs, after which mother and embryo would be thrown into the crematorium.

Gisella Perl decided to warn the women of the danger. She would abort every pregnancy she could in order to save the mothers' lives. In addition to the abortions, she was one of five doctors at Auschwitz who were supposed to operate a hospital ward with no beds, bandages, drugs, or medical instruments. She had to try to heal the many diseases brought on by torture, starvation, and filth. She had to treat broken bones and heads that had been cracked by vicious beatings. The only "medicine" she had to offer was the spoken word. She would tell her patients that one day life would be good again.

When she was liberated, she wandered through Germany on foot, searching for her family. She quickly learned that her husband had been beaten to death just before liberation and her teenage son had died in a gas chamber. She herself then succumbed to grief and tried to kill herself with poison. Unsuccessful, she was taken to a convent in France to recuperate.

In 1947, Dr. Perl came to the United States to speak to doctors about the horrors she had seen. One day she met Eleanor Roosevelt and they had lunch together. The former first lady told her, "Stop torturing yourself. Become a doctor again." With the help of a local congressman, she opened an office in Manhattan and joined the staff at Mt. Sinai Hospital. There she became an expert in treating fertility and delivered three thousand babies. In her seventies she moved to Jerusalem and donated her time to the gynecological clinic at Shaarei Zedek Hospital, helping women to give birth.

Whenever she entered a delivery room, after she began to deliver babies again following the war, she would always first stop to utter her own special prayer: "God, you owe me a life, a living baby."

Gisella Perl knew firsthand despair and fear. But she also was able to draw on a wellspring of hope and faith. She was a living embodiment of courage.

There indeed is wisdom in the art of facing fear. Dr. Remen asks us, "How do we need to live so that we do not die overcome with fear and anxiety?" Dr. Dennis Gersten teaches us to face our fear, not push it away. Hamilton Jordan shows us a way to work through our fear. And Gisella Perl makes a deal with God to continue to live with hope, telling God, "You owe me a life, a living baby."

I hope that the examples of such people can help us live the rest of our lives with a greater hope in the future and in our own abilities.

The Faith in Fear

There is a harshness to life that cannot be ignored. We will know fear and anxiety. But even though we cannot always change reality, we can change how we view reality. Or at least we can give it a good try. We can struggle with a faith that tells us that we are never alone, that even in our darkest night, God is with us, to comfort us and help us reach the light.

17

Abandon Revenge and Resentment

A few years ago advice columnist Ann Landers passed away. With her death a genuine source of wisdom and insight left us, and those of us who read her column occasionally miss her advice. But it was not only in her answers that wisdom was found. Sometimes the letters to Ann were also important sources of perspective. For instance, consider this letter sent to Ann on the subject of forgiving abusive parents:

> Yes, my parents were abusive, both verbally and physically. They never bothered to control their tempers, and they took out their frustrations on each other and on us children....

Having said this, the letter writer then proceeds to say that she has forgiven her parents nevertheless. She explains:

> Forgiveness is a great healer. I no longer hold feelings of anger over what happened to me as a child. There is a great deal of freedom in forgiving. I can achieve any goal I wish without the shackles of blame. I have no score to settle with my parents. I don't keep a tally of wrongs done to me by them. I awake every morning free and unchained.

The writer concludes:

Life is so very, very short. Why spend time on negative
thoughts? They only hurt the person who feels them. If you
must have revenge, then forgive. That is the best revenge of all.

The Temptation of Revenge

In chapter 3, I wrote about forgiveness, and the basic message was
this: Forgiveness is for the person offended, not for the offender. It
allows us to let go of our negative thoughts and move on, even if the
other person is not cooperating. I still heartily believe that, when it
comes to most hurts we suffer, this message is correct. But the continuing onslaughts of terror in Israel and, of course, the aftermath of
9/11 have forced me to consider that there may be times when letting
go of our pain is not the best choice. In certain circumstances, something beyond forgiveness may be required, something that sounds
most un-PC, even biblical in its perspective. I am speaking of the
concept of revenge.

Revenge is not something I typically endorse; indeed, I have casti-
gated those bent on revenge. But there is a seductive appeal in getting
even, and at no time in my life has such an appeal tempted me as it
does these days. I wanted revenge on Osama Bin Laden. I wanted
revenge on Hamas. I wanted revenge on Yasir Arafat. While I'm at
it, I am sure there is a list somewhere in the darker part of my brain
of people who have personally wronged me. Forgiveness has been
my modus operandi, but I would be lying if I didn't admit continued
hopes that somehow those who maligned my character will meet a
poetically just fate, preferably one I will get to witness.

There is a tale of the Lithuanian Yiddish character Khabad,
whose house caught fire. When the house was going up in flames,
instead of running around in a panic, as his neighbors were doing, he
began to laugh. "At last," he exclaimed, "I have my revenge on my
cockroaches." This absurd need for revenge can be self-destructive at

worst and at best not pretty to watch, but pondering it cannot help but feel good, doesn't it?

I recently heard the story of a woman at the store checkout. "Cash, check, or charge?" asked the clerk, after folding items the woman wished to purchase. As she fumbled for her wallet, the clerk noticed a remote control for a television set in her purse.

"Do you always carry your TV remote?" asked the clerk.

"No," she replied. "But my husband refused to come shopping with me, so I figured this was the most evil thing I could do to him."

All kidding aside, revenge is no laughing matter. A few years ago I read a book by Laura Blumenfeld, improbably titled: *Revenge: A Story of Hope*. In the book, the author describes her attempt to avenge a Palestinian terrorist attack against her father. Years before, her father, an American Conservative rabbi, had been walking in the Old City of Jerusalem when he was shot by an agent of a Palestinian faction opposed to the PLO. Fortunately, her father survived the incident intact. But the author could not forget this injustice. After the shooting, she fantasized about what it would be like to take vengeance on the shooter.

Years later the daughter spent her honeymoon year in Israel and incongruously resolved to confront her father's attacker. She imagined seeing the shooter, reaching out through the darkness, grabbing his collar, shaking him hard. She knew this wish was only a fantasy. What she really wanted to understand was the power of revenge. We all have dark thoughts. But what if we pursue them?

The Lessons Beyond Revenge

Research into revenge reveals that it is not uncommon for societies to have laws forbidding revenge while at the same time having customs that promote revenge. Judaism is typical. We are told in Leviticus not to seek vengeance (19:18), but in Exodus we read, "An eye for an eye, a tooth for a tooth" (21:24). Which is right?

In America, revenge is harbored in families for years, at least if your name is Hatfield or McCoy. In the Middle East, nomadic Bedouins have a saying that reflects their ability to hold cross-generational grudges: "If a man takes revenge after forty years, he was in a hurry."

Armed with this knowledge, Laura Blumenfeld explored first-hand her feelings by actually befriending the family of the shooter. She posed as a non-Jewish writer doing a story on revenge. By the end of the book, when she dramatically reveals her true identity in a courtroom, she has learned something about her personal need for revenge. She did not want to punish the shooter or his family. She wanted to teach them a lesson. As she tells the judge, her motive for deceiving the family was educational: "I wanted them to understand this conflict is between human beings and not disembodied Arabs and Jews," she explained. "We're people. Not 'targets.' We're people with families. And you can't just kill us."[1]

Laura Blumenfeld's story has a happy ending in that she shares her humanity with the shooter and his family. They came to see the divinity in each other. The shooter is still in prison, but he is no longer a terrorist. And the victim's daughter can let go of her pain. Her figurative prison sentence is over.

Interestingly enough, the Torah has a similar story of revenge versus education. In Genesis 42, when Joseph's brothers go down to Egypt, Joseph immediately recognizes them. He remembers how they kidnapped him and sent him as a slave to Egypt. But Joseph's brothers don't recognize Joseph. Instead of telling them his identity, Joseph is very harsh to them. Some readers see this as Joseph exacting revenge. But careful readers understand that Joseph is not seeking vengeance. He is testing his brothers to see if they have changed, if they are still capable of such an evil act. Ultimately, he teaches them how they should behave. Like Laura Blumenfeld, Joseph uses deception and personal pain for a good cause.

Resentment—The Other Burden

Fortunately, most of us will not have such a dramatic decision to make regarding vengeance. We will not be victims of major crimes, and for those who are, we hope that society will mete out justice. But all of us will be victims of the inappropriate behavior of others, and we will be tempted to bear grudges. We will have to choose between the quick fix of getting even—seductive but harmful to our souls—and the refreshing force of integrity. We reclaim the power over our lives by not giving in to the temptation to get even.

When that time comes, I hope we will be guided by the examples of others and the wisdom of our tradition. Regarding vengeance, consider the guidance of the Rabbis in the Talmud: The Torah teaches, "You shall not hate your neighbor in your heart" (Leviticus 19:17). For one might think: I must not strike him or beat him or curse him, but I may hate him. Thus it teaches, "in your heart." It's not enough to avoid striking back. We must also learn to let go of our resentment.

Of course, this is not easy to do, even when it comes to the small injustices we suffer. When people wrong us, we naturally resent them for it. We resent their taking advantage of us. We resent their telling us no when we want to hear yes. We resent their not treating us the same way we would treat them. Left unchecked, this resentment can grow, much as a cancerous tumor grows. And like a tumor, as it grows we become sicker and sicker. As we noted in chapter 3, the word *resentment* actually means "to keep feeling the same emotion over and over again—re-sentiment." It's not a very pleasant thing. When we let go of this resentment, we rid ourselves of the bitterness that keeps us from enjoying life fully.

This can happen on a personal level, when we reach out to alienated friends or estranged family members and try to restore the relationship, but it also can happen in the international sphere. Consider, for example, the actions of General Douglas MacArthur. At the end of World War II, after the Japanese surrendered, MacArthur asked President Harry S. Truman to allow him to stay in Japan. He wanted to help restore the dignity of the Japanese people. He wanted to assist them in getting their country back on its feet after our atomic bombs had leveled the cities of Hiroshima and Nagasaki.

Something in the heart of Douglas MacArthur prompted him to step back into that place of devastation and help those who had been our enemies. While many (or most?) in America entertained thoughts of revenge, MacArthur took a different tack. They need a government that works, he suggested. They need their dignity. They need hope. They need new strength to go on and rebuild. When Douglas MacArthur chose to head up the reconciliation with Japan, the work must not have been easy, but it allowed both countries to move forward together.

A very dramatic example of such difficult—but vital—work is recorded by Jay Winik in his Civil War saga *April 1865: The Month That Saved America*. In the late spring of 1865, the country was just beginning to heal. On a warm Sunday at St. Paul's Episcopal Church in Richmond, Virginia, an older man, one of the church's many distinguished congregants, was sitting in his customary pew. He had spent the last four years at war. With his shoulders rounded, his middle thickened, his hair snow-white, and his beard gray, he attracted the attention of the rest of the church. But so did another parishioner on that morning.

As the minister was about to administer Holy Communion, a tall, well-dressed black man, sitting in the gallery reserved for black worshippers, unexpectedly advanced to the communion table. This had never happened before. In the Richmond of prewar years, whites always received communion first, and then blacks. To alter this ritual was unthinkable. The congregation froze; those who had been poised to go forward and kneel at the altar rail remained fixed in their pews. The minister was clearly embarrassed and did nothing. It was one thing for the white South to endure defeat and poverty or to accept that slaves were now free; it was quite another for a black man to stride up to the front of the church as though he were an equal. This was not just any church. This was the sanctuary for Richmond's elite, the wealthy, the well-bred, the high-cultured. The black man slowly lowered his body, kneeling, while the rest of the congregation tensed in their pews. The minister stood dumbfounded. After what seemed to be an interminable amount of time—although it was probably only seconds—the white man back from the war arose, head up and eyes proud, and walked quietly up the aisle to the chancel rail.

> His face was a portrait of exhaustion, and he looked far older than most people had remembered when the war had just begun. These days had been [especially] hard on him.... Yet these Richmonders, like all of the South, still looked to him for a sense of purpose and guidance. No less now as, with quiet dignity and self-possession, he knelt down to partake of the communion, along the same rail with the black man.[2]

Who was this old soldier who was willing to cross the lines and move forward from hatred and revenge to reconciliation? It was Robert E. Lee, and it can be said that, more than any other time, when he went forward to kneel beside that black man, the Civil War was finally over.

Letting Go of Pain and Hurt

I know that, especially these days, we have the right to feel anger over the actions of others. We have the right to seek vengeance. In the traditional Yom Kippur morning liturgy, we read of the rabbinic martyrs, murdered by the Romans two thousand years ago. In our time we could add to the list the victims of suicide bombs in Israel, 9/11 in America, and the slain American journalist Daniel Pearl. Certainly we hope that the perpetrators of these heinous acts are brought to justice. But I also hope that we are able to see that our world and our own spiritual selves will be better off the more we are able to let go of the pain and move on with our lives. In the Bible, this is what Joseph does. When he names his son Menashe, which means "to cause to forget," he declares that God has made him completely forget his hardship. Did Joseph really forget? Of course not. He simply let go of the painful part of the memory. We could learn from Joseph.

When there is a prospect of reconciliation, by all means let us consider pursuing it. Who knows, maybe this will be the year we come clean with the family members we've been avoiding. This will be the year the person who ignores us will decide she owes us a second chance or at least a conversation about why she is so angry. Maybe this year we will discover that life is too short and the world too small for us to give up on each other.

18

Finish the Race
You Started

Georgene Johnson lived in Cleveland. She was forty-two years old and she was trying to have a good attitude about being forty-two years old. So she started running and exercising to keep in shape. She said, "I'm not going to look like I am forty-two, or at least I am going to look like a good forty-two."

She did well in her running. She was running farther every day. She thought she would try a little competition and entered a 10K race. That's about six miles. Nervous about her first race, she got up early and arrived at the start of the race. To her surprise, there were a lot of people milling around, stretching, getting ready. All of a sudden a voice on the microphone said, "Move to the starting line." This was it. A gun sounded and they were off like a huge wave—hundreds of runners, sweeping her along. She was in the race.

After about four miles, it occurred to her that they ought to be turning around and heading back to the finish line. She wondered why they hadn't turned around. She stopped and asked an official, "How come the course isn't turning around?" He said, "Ma'am, you are running the Cleveland Marathon." Twenty-six miles. Her event, the 10K, was set to begin a half-hour after the start of the marathon.

Some of us would have stopped right there and said, "That's it, I'm going home." But to her credit, Georgene Johnson kept right on going and finished the race. Afterwards, she said, "This is not the race I trained for. This is not the race I entered. But for better or worse, this is the race that I am in."

Life's Full of Surprises

I am sure many of us have had the same experience, if not in a marathon, then facing one of life's many surprise challenges. Was it a relationship that morphed into something different? Was it a job that became precarious because of new economic realities? Was it an unexpected health concern? Consider divorce, sickness, the debilitation of old age, disease—we never imagine it is going to happen to us.

All of us face situations that are not of our making and that frighten us, frustrate us, and even anger us. In this regard, we are not so different from Moses in the Torah. After all, he started his life as a prince in Egypt. Later, after he signed up as God's right-hand man, he must have considered the fringe benefits as equal to the task. Imagine these perks: immediate access to God 24/7, eternal fame, and unquestioned authority! Readers of the Torah know that things didn't quite turn out that way. The people questioned Moses's leadership for forty years. God was often an absentee boss. And more than once Moses expressed exasperation with the burden of leadership.

But he never gave up. He continued the race, even though it was not the one he had entered. Why not quit? Was it his character? His faith in the ultimate goodness of God? The awareness that people were depending on him? Maybe it was all these things and one more thought as well: Maybe Moses simply didn't want to quit. He wanted to finish the race.

The Four Mandates for Finishing

None of us is called on to be Moses. But each of us is called to finish the race we've started. It's not only that we don't want to be quitters.

It's also that people are counting on us. Maybe we feel that we are obligated to God as well. After all, our lives are a divine gift. What gives us the right to dictate the character of that gift?

So let's assume that we are going to finish the race we started. Fortunately, help is out there, by way of good advice. Runners have their shared wisdom, as do all athletes. But what about participants in a spiritual race?

I have found that such a challenge is made easier by remembering four things to do as we race ahead. Why four? Well, for one thing, it is a good Jewish number. Think about Passover—four cups of wine, four sons, four questions. There are also the four matriarchs. In addition, four is about the highest number of things we can remember without writing them down. And who goes running with pockets anyway?

In any case, here they are. Four mandates for finishing the race:

Show up.

Be present.

Be yourself.

Let go.

Show Up

We all know that showing up is key. Getting there, no matter what the speed, is not everything, but it matters a lot. As Woody Allen first declared, "Ninety percent of success is just showing up."

Make no mistake: This is not the world in which I would have chosen to "show up." Who among us, after reading the morning newspaper or watching the evening news, doesn't feel as "one untimely born"? This is what lay behind novelist Joseph Heller's preface in the early editions of *Catch-22* with this warning/confession: "All events in the book were based on reality, but have been changed to make them more believable."

We really do live in an unbelievable world. Think about how crazy contemporary life is. Our world doesn't make sense. We are polluting ourselves to death. Each day seems to bring word of more senseless death and terror. There is enough food produced throughout the world to provide sufficient nutrition for each person on the planet, yet hundreds of thousands of people die each year of starvation and more than a billion people on our planet are significantly malnourished. It's the fault of humans, not nature. Millions of people are suffering from diseases for which we have cures. Poverty-stricken countries aren't able to buy vaccines to prevent polio, measles, and yellow fever or to provide drugs to cure tuberculosis or leprosy.

The United States is the wealthiest nation on Earth, but more than 11 million American children live below the poverty level. Many of our schools fail to do their jobs. We say the future depends on our children, but we spend so little time with them. We pay their teachers a tiny percentage of what we pay professional athletes. Too many of our students suffer in poorly run schools open to gangs and fellow students packing weapons.

We make celebrities of people who betray their spouses or children. People who commit outrageous acts become guests on television talk shows. To put it plainly, the world doesn't make sense. Yet this is the world we have been given. Our first response is to show up.

Be Present

Showing up is important, but we also have to be present. Anyone who has faithfully shown up and then blissfully slept through 8:00 a.m. chemistry lectures, Monday morning staff meetings, Friday afternoon faculty meetings, and Friday night worship services knows that sometimes showing up just isn't enough. We must also genuinely be present—a state of what the Quakers call "all-there-ness." Give the moment everything you've got. Give life all of yourself. Be fully in the moment. Whatever you are doing, do it with full awareness.

One of the worst things you can do in life—just as when you're driving a car—is fall asleep at the wheel. Life takes our complete concentration; we must become masters of an undivided attention to living. *Be present* also means being alert to the possibilities of helping others and not allowing our parochial concerns to blind us to their needs.

Be Yourself

After being present, the third mandate is to be yourself. There is an old piece of advice a professor at rabbinical school used to give us. He would say, "The most important thing in life is to be yourself. Unless you are a jerk. Then be someone else." All humor aside, what he meant was that many of us would try to be the carbon copy of some rabbinic mentor, instead of being the best original. Likewise for all of us, God wants us to be who we are. An old cowboy saying declares, "You can put a boot in the oven, but it won't come out a biscuit." Each of us must make our own biscuit from scratch, using the energy, talents, skills, guts, and gifts God has given us.

To "be yourself" requires that you first know who you are, and that takes a lifetime of work. You don't "just grow." No one "just grows." We all grow in certain ways that God intends or doesn't intend. Into whose image will you "grow"? Will you grow into God's image and God's image for you, or will you grow into God's image for someone else and someone else's image?

There is a famous Hasidic story about Rabbi Zusya of Hanipol, who lay on his deathbed with tears streaming down his face.

His disciples asked, "Why are you crying?"

Rabbi Zusya answered, "If God asks me why I wasn't like Moses or Maimonides, I'll say, I wasn't blessed with that kind of leadership ability and wisdom. But I'm afraid of another question. What if God asks, 'Rabbi Zusya, why weren't you like Rabbi Zusya? Why didn't you find your inner being and realize your inner potential? Why didn't you find yourself?' That is why I am crying."

Let Go

The fourth mandate, following show up, be present, and be yourself, is *let go*. It is also, of course, the main idea of this book.

William Holmes Border, a Baptist preacher, liked to pray before church services, "Lord, let something happen here today that's not in the bulletin." He knew that genuine spirituality emerges in unplanned moments. But he also knew that the willingness to "let go" is difficult, as any parent can tell you. The wonderful surprise that God has in store for us is that when we can at last "let go" and let God take control, we do not suddenly experience some sort of stomach-squeezing free fall but a liberating freedom from fallenness. In other words, paradoxically, we are only liberated when we realize that we are not in control.

There's one secular institution out there that seems to understand this paradox. The business world is moving from a control paradigm to a trust paradigm. In this age of heightened accountability, it's tempting to try to manipulate the system to bring about our desired ends. The world is too complicated for that to work, however. Therefore, the smarter choice is to practice wise relinquishment: Learn to do what you can, and then let go.

By letting go we do not give up the race. We simply recognize that we were never in control of the path of the course; that is, how we were going to get to the finish line. We are never running alone. The best runners realize that there are many factors beyond their control; even so, they have many wellsprings of support to draw from.

19

Hold on Tightly, Let Go Lightly

A great Hasidic master told a parable of a father, a merchant who once took his young son with him on a business trip. They passed through a thick forest, where the boy spied beautiful blackberries, and he very much wanted to stop and pick them. The father told his son that he could not stop, that business was pressing, and that they must continue riding.

The son said to him, "Let me get off and gather my berries while you ride onward slowly. Do not worry; I will find you."

"But my son," the father replied, "I fear that you will be lost."

"Well," said the son, "every now and then I will call to you and you can answer me. When I have finished picking my berries I will come along and join you."

As the son left the wagon to go into the forest, the father told him, "Remember, my son, if you hear the voice of your father and follow it, all will be well and you will not get lost. But if you do not listen, you will not hear my voice. And once you no longer hear the voice of your father, you will remain lost in this great and forbidding forest."

We, too, are quite busy with the berries of life, grabbing as much as we can of the petty material luxuries available to us. And as the father warned, we no longer listen for the voice of God, and we find ourselves spiritually lost.

In a metaphor remarkably similar to that of the Hasidic master's parable, the poet Elizabeth Barrett Browning, in her poem "Aurora Leigh," put it this way:

> *Earth's crammed with heaven,*
> *And every common bush afire with God;*
> *But only he who sees, takes off his shoes;*
> *the rest sit round it and pluck blackberries.*

Trapped by Our Own Doing

Why are we so distant when it comes to relating to God? It's tempting to blame it on bad, immature theology that creates so much dissonance between the idea of a traditional reward-and-punishment God and the loving God in which we long to believe. But there is another, simpler reason why we are so distant from God: When it comes to searching for God, we are otherwise engaged.

Here is a fascinating fact. Native hunters in the jungles of Africa have a clever way of trapping monkeys. They slice a coconut in two, hollow it out, and in one half of the shell they cut a hole just big enough for a monkey's hand to pass through. Then they place an orange in the other coconut half before fastening together the two halves of the coconut shell. Finally, they secure the coconut to a tree with a rope, retreat into the jungle, and wait.

Sooner or later, an unsuspecting monkey swings by, smells the delicious orange, and discovers its location inside the coconut. The monkey then slips his hand through the small hole, grasps the orange and tries to pull it out the hole. Of course the orange won't come out; it's too big for the hole. To no avail the persistent monkey continues to pull and pull, never realizing the danger he is in.

While the monkey struggles with the orange, the hunters simply stroll in and capture the monkey by throwing a net over him. As long as the monkey keeps his fist wrapped around the orange, the monkey is trapped.

Scientists have always contended that monkeys are among the most intelligent animals on the face of the Earth. If this is true, then the monkey is surely smart enough to know that the way to escape the trap is very simple. Just by letting go of its hold on the orange, it would be able to free itself, but it chooses not to do so. The monkey could save its own life if it would only let go of the orange. Yet it rarely occurs to a monkey that it can't have both the orange and its freedom. That delicious orange becomes a deadly trap.

The world sets traps for us that are not unlike the monkey trap. We constantly hear that if we just have enough possessions, enough status, enough power, and enough prestige, we'd be happy. Under that illusion, people spend their whole lives trying to pull the orange out of the coconut. Yet the truth is deceptively simple: We have to let it go so we can get unstuck!

Yes, it is a paradox: In order to hold on to what matters most in life, we have to learn to let go of our trappings.

Letting Go Brings Growth and Meaning

Hold on tightly, let go lightly. This is a well-known mantra but its simplicity is profound.

It calls us to cherish each moment that we have but to know that it's fleeting. By denying this, we become ensnared by our own desires for things. We close ourselves off from experiencing the very essence of life.

Letting go doesn't mean giving up on improving ourselves and the world. It doesn't mean relinquishing our responsibilities to God, and it doesn't mean putting the blame on others. Letting go doesn't mean escaping the real world. But all of us hold on tightly to things that have no business accompanying us on our journeys. Indeed, such possessions must be identified and abandoned if we truly wish to grow as human beings.

The heaviest burden we carry is our fear of death. To be human means to fear death, and reading a hundred million books will not change the fact that we're going to die or even rid us of our fear of death. But if we see ourselves for who we are instead of what we have, if we recognize that we are more than the sum of our material goods, then maybe death will mean something different to us. If we realize that our essential selves are not exclusively defined by what we have, our approach to death may change.

Once a beloved Indian saint was dying and the people said to him, "Don't leave us! Don't leave us!" He said, "Don't be silly, where could I go?" Somehow this man understood that his finite existence on Earth did not correspond to his immortal essence, his true being. While holding on tightly to life and all its gifts, he could let go lightly of them because they *were* gifts. Or more precisely, borrowed gifts. As the book of Ecclesiastes reminds us, everything we enjoy is a gift from God (5:18).

To let go of our fear of death doesn't mean to pretend that there is no pain at the end of life or in losing loved ones who go before us. Letting go means refusing to spend our days in fear and refusing to allow our fear to color everything we do while we live.

Because we're afraid of death, our society has an obsession with trying to ignore it. As a result, we live our lives as if our days were not numbered. We fear that our acknowledgment that life is finite would somehow rob our days of meaning. So we do not talk about it and try not to think about it. Yet accepting the inevitability of death can do just the opposite—it can lead us to a much richer life. Death can give life meaning. Albert Schweitzer once observed:

> We must all become familiar with the thought of death if we want to grow into really good people. We need not think of it every day or every hour.... [But thinking] about death ... produces love for life. When we are familiar with death, we accept each week, each day, as a gift. Only if we are able thus to accept life—bit by bit—does it become precious.[1]

Dzevad Sabanagic, the leader of a string quartet in Sarajevo, understood what Dr. Schweitzer meant. When asked by a reporter to describe his experience living with war back in the 1990s, he replied, "Every time I left home, when grenades were falling, I knew that I could die. I always thought when I got to the concert hall that this might be the last time I played. So I thought I'd play with all my heart."[2]

As survivors of war understand all too well, our days here are numbered. Life is a gift that must be returned. Instead of denying this truth or fearing it, this knowledge can lead us to a wonderful appreciation of life. It can help us hold on tightly, even as we know that we must let go lightly.

Remember, as the Jewish people have always believed, God will never abandon us. Given God, all that we cherish can pass away into hands better, stronger, and wiser than our own. Life is dear, but it must not be held too dearly. The American Pulitzer Prize–winning poet Edna St. Vincent Millay wrote, "O world I cannot hold thee close enough." But our days must be filled with letting go, with giving up what never really belonged to us in the first place.

20

Open Up
Your Eyes

One night a burglar broke into a house. He shined his flashlight around, looking for valuables, and when he picked up an iPad to place in his sack, a strange, disembodied voice echoed from the dark, "God is watching you."

The burglar nearly jumped out of his skin. He clicked his flashlight off and froze. After a few minutes, when he heard nothing more, he shook his head, promised himself a vacation after the next big score, then clicked the light back on and began searching for more valuables. Just as he pulled the flat-screen TV out so he could disconnect the wires, clear as a bell he heard, "God is watching you."

Freaked out, he shined his light around frantically, looking for the source of the voice. Finally, in the corner of the room, his flashlight beam came to rest on a parrot. "Did you say that?" he hissed at the parrot.

"Yep," the parrot confessed, then squawked. "I am just trying to warn you."

The burglar relaxed. "Warn me, huh? Who the heck are you?"

"Moses," replied the bird.

"Moses?" the burglar laughed. "What kind of stupid people would name a parrot Moses?"

The bird promptly answered, "Probably the same kind of people who would name a Rottweiler God."

Defining Our View

As this story reminds us, most religions—including Judaism—teach that God is always watching us. In modern times, God's constant attention is a subject of debate. This may be the wrong issue, however. What may be more important for us is not the question of what God sees but, rather, what we see. In other words, how do we view the world? What do we see when we greet the day? What is our perspective? Our attitude?

A famous story in Genesis 21 deals with just this call to attention. In the tale, traditionally read in the synagogue on Rosh Hashanah, Hagar and her son, Ishmael, have been sent out of the camp because Sarah doesn't want them around her beloved Isaac. The two appear destined to die in the wilderness. And then we read:

> And the water was spent in the bottle, and she cast the child under one of the shrubs. And she went, and sat down opposite him a good way off, a bowshot away; for she said, "Let me not see the death of the child." And she sat opposite him, and lifted up her voice, and wept. And God heard the voice of the lad; and the angel of God called to Hagar from heaven, and said to her, "What ails you, Hagar? Fear not; for God has heard the voice of the lad where he is. Arise, lift up the lad, and hold him in your hand; for I will make him a great nation." God opened her eyes, and she saw a well of water; and she went, and filled the bottle with water, and gave the lad to drink. God was with the lad; and he grew, and lived in the wilderness, and became an archer. (Genesis 21:15–20)

To me, the key words of the story are these: "God opened her eyes, and she saw a well of water." Think about it. Was the well of water magically produced or was it there all the time? Answer: It was there all the time; Hagar was just too busy to notice the well. God did not literally open up her eyes; God inspired her to use her eyes to see reality.

Missing the Miracles

In the last few years, a new song has been sung in Reform Jewish circles. Written by Cantor Jeff Klepper, it goes like this:

> *Open up our eyes, teach us how to live,*
> *Fill our hearts with joy and all the love you have to give.*
> *Gather us in peace as you lead us to Your Name,*
> *And we will know that You are One.*

I have been intrigued by the first line: "Open up our eyes, teach us how to live." How does God teach us how to live? The answer: By opening up our eyes. So much of our Jewish wisdom can be simplified into this one command: Open up our eyes.

The song pleads to God to open up our eyes. The problem isn't that we are blind. The problem is that many of us simply can't see what is in front of us. There are wellsprings of life around us and we just don't see them. It's not that we don't take our eyesight seriously. In fact, most of us are very conscientious about improving our diminishing eyesight. I recently read that more than a million Americans every year agree to let an ophthalmologist take a small excimer knife, called a microkeratome, and cut the flap of the cornea so that a laser can be used to change the shape of the cornea. If the procedure is successful, there is no need to wear contacts or eyeglasses anymore, and overall vision is improved.

This procedure helps millions of people see better. But here is the irony. Even after the surgery, even for those of us with 20/20 vision, even on the darkest days, our world is full of light that we still cannot see. Our human eyes are designed to detect only visible light, which is a tiny sliver of the electromagnetic spectrum, the part made up of light with relatively short wavelengths. All other forms of light are completely invisible to us. It's there right before us, but we can't see it.

This is the very type of seeing hinted at in the story of Hagar. It's not about laser surgery. It's about having eyes that don't let us take for granted—or miss—the pleasures of life.

So why don't we perceive them? Why do we ignore this light around us?

Replacing Our Lenses

Perhaps we need a whole new way of seeing—an eye transplant. God knows that our usual eyes are not good enough. They fail us in so many ways. The eyes of cynicism are not working for us. We have a hard time believing that people can live authentic lives of compassion and selflessness, and this colors the way we choose to live our own lives. It affects our belief in a loving and caring Providence. It leaves us bitter and feeling that the world has given us short shrift, that life has unfairly passed us by. The eyes of envy fail us, too, making whatever we own never enough, and leading us to judge others—and ourselves—by our possessions.

The truth is, we have never had it so good. Compared to a couple of centuries ago, we have everything: modern medicine, communication devices, electricity. We are cleaner, healthier, more in touch with each other, but we are not happier. Part of the problem is that we look at the world through eyes that confuse the good with the "goods," but the goods never adequately deliver.

The eyes of rationalism aren't much better. We think that there's nothing real except the visible world. Unless we can see it, touch it, taste it, hear it, or smell it, it's not there. It's hard for us to believe that there's an unseen God who cares about us. We want a God who is manageable, understandable, visible—a God who shows up once in a while. But that's not the God we are going to find.

The eyes of narcissism definitely aren't working. "Doing our own thing" doesn't serve us as well as we once thought. There's an old observation that still hits home: The most popular magazine used to be the one called *Life*. All of life. That was succeeded by *People*.

Not all of life, but at least all people. Then *People* was challenged on newsstands by *Us*. Not even all people—just us. And now we see on the newsstand a magazine called *Self*. Where might we go from here? Certainly not to a place of insight.

Of course, many of us are pretty enlightened people. We are not cynical, we don't let envy ruin us, and we appreciate the mystical elements of life. We even value other people. Even so, I would challenge us to consider how we might also spiritually see better. If a transplant isn't needed, perhaps we simply need a new prescription. We need a lens that will enable us to see what we've never seen before. If we changed our lenses, what might we improve? I am no ophthalmologist, but I have a few suggestions for new lenses we should wear. Consider these changes:

- It may be the lens of Torah. If we pledge ourselves to study the precious wisdom of our heritage, we'll see better. Take a class. Find a resource online. Buy and read a Jewish book. Let Torah study be our new lens.

- It may be the lens of the synagogue. We need the encouragement and support of a family of families, of a congregation who cares about each other.

- It may be the lens of worship. We need to feed our souls so that the eyes of faith will remain healthy. Worship is not merely about coming to synagogue and saying ancient words. It is about achieving a better perspective, a clearer vision. I recently read about a couple who went to see the Wild Animal Park in San Diego. Since there was so much to see, they were tempted to rush through the park. But they decided to give the birds more time, even if it meant missing something else. As they later discovered, "The longer you sit still, the more you see." The longer they sat, the more they noticed the different kinds of birds, hidden because of their camouflage colors. They also noticed new birds, which only came out after the couple stayed still.

- It may be the lens of service, of doing *mitzvot*. We need to get outside of ourselves to give our time to others. Removing the focus from ourselves to others will make the eyes of faith much stronger.

The good news for us is that eyes that see the blessings of the world are not given to us at birth. They are developed over a lifetime of looking. And we can all develop them.

Peer Past the Obstacles

Someone once wrote, "I am not surprised at what people suffer, but I am surprised at what people miss." There is so much we miss of the world because we do not see clearly. Making room for what matters most means refocusing our eyes on the things we should be seeing, as opposed to the things that get in our way. A newspaper reported the story of a mother who was taking her young son to Salt Lake City on a melancholy mission. The boy had lost the sight of one of his eyes several years before, and in the intervening years doctors had tried valiantly to save his remaining eye. Now they had come to the reluctant conclusion that the eye could not be saved. Before the darkness set in, his mother wanted the boy to have a fond lingering look at the majestic mountains of Utah so that he could take that splendid image with him into the sightless future. Can we hear such a story without becoming aware of how many visual marvels beckon to us and that we persistently overlook?

King David once said to God, "Open my eyes, that I may see" (Psalm 119:18). Our song says, "Open up our eyes, teach us how to live." It would be good for all of us to see more clearly the miracles before us, the opportunities that await us, and the presence of God always with us. Is God watching us? I honestly don't know. But we could do a better job seeing the world. We do so by focusing on the right things to see.

21

Write Your Name Upon the Hearts of Others

"**H**ow were the receipts today in Madison Square Garden?" This sounds like a simple question, deserving of a simple answer, and yet it turned out to be the final words of the world-famous circus promoter P. T. Barnum. The man spoke these words, then passed away. Some famous last words! "How were the receipts today in Madison Square Garden?" It is sad but true that the last words of history's great people are rarely inspiring, and they are usually about as interesting and uplifting as the phone book.

We want pearls of profound wisdom from our dying artists, authors, and world leaders, but we rarely get them. Consider these examples:

- Mexican revolutionary hero Francisco "Pancho" Villa uttered to a comrade, "Don't let it end this way. Tell them I said something."

- Legendary poet Lord Byron came up with this: "Now I shall go to sleep. Good-night."

- Johann Wolfgang von Goethe couldn't do better than "Open the second shutter so that more light may come in." Apparently, his editors found these words to be so dismally

dull that they trimmed the sentence down to the inspirational phrase, "More light!"

• Marie Antoinette, the doomed queen of France, was clumsy
but polite: "*Pardonnez-moi, Monsieur,*" she said, after inad-
vertently stepping on her executioner's toe.

For pure entertainment value, you can't beat the last words of some
condemned prisoners, especially if you have a taste for graveyard
humor. A criminal named James Roges was asked by the firing squad
commander if he had a last request. "Why, yes," said the clever con-
vict. "A bulletproof vest!" And you've got to feel some admiration
for a condemned murderer who can continue to crack jokes from the
electric chair. "How about this for a headline in tomorrow's paper?"
James French said. "French Fries!"

My personal favorite is from General John Sedgwick, the Union
commander killed in battle during the Civil War in 1864: "They
couldn't hit an elephant at this dist ..." Or there is the admirable gram-
matical devotion in the last words of French grammarian Dominique
Bouhours: "I am about to—or I am going to—die; either expression
is used."

Of course, some might argue that dying words need not be profound as long as they are honest. Zen master Suzuki Roshi's dying was
described by Natalie Goldberg in her book *Writing Down the Bones*.
Goldberg writes:

> He died of cancer in 1971. When Zen masters die we like to
> think they will say something very inspiring as they are about
> to bite the Big Emptiness, something like "Hi-ho Silver!" or
> "Remember to wake up" or "Life is everlasting." Right before
> Suzuki's death, Katagiri Roshi, an old friend, visited him.
> Katagiri stood by the bedside; Suzuki looked up and said, "I
> don't want to die."[1]

That simple. He was who he was and said plainly what he felt in the moment. We might have expected more from a great Buddhist master, but what could be greater than honesty when facing death?

Whenever I speak of mortality, I am reminded of the rabbi who announced on Yom Kippur that everyone in the congregation will one day die. All grew silent and reflected on this painful truth. But one man in the front started laughing. The rabbi couldn't help stopping and saying to the man, "What's so funny? Didn't you hear what I said? Everyone in the congregation will die." To which the man replied, smiling, "But I'm not a member!"

Sharing the Lifeboat with Death

The bad news is, whether we pay our temple dues are not, our lifetime membership will one day expire. So how do we respond? To be human is to fear death. But how do we deal with that fear? This is no easy task. It's recorded that the great tycoon William Randolph Hearst had so powerful a fear of death that the very mention of the word in his presence was strictly forbidden. Even in his newspapers the subject had to be handled very carefully. Ernst Becker, in his classic book *The Denial of Death,* points out that the fear of death haunts the human animal like nothing else. And it is universal in the human condition.

When it comes to thinking about death, no one is an expert, least of all me. Yet this is a subject that must be addressed, because it is so crucial to who we are as human beings. A vital insight comes not from a Jewish text, although the idea is found in Jewish tradition, but from a powerful novel. *The Life of Pi,* by Yann Martel, is the story of a young teenage boy who is stuck in the middle of the Pacific Ocean on a small lifeboat. Unfortunately, he must share this small home with a 450-pound Bengal tiger! Pi, the sole human survivor of a cargo ship that sinks in the Pacific Ocean, accidentally rescues the tiger. Pi had been traveling with his family and animals from his family's zoo in India to Canada, where they hoped to start a new life. For 227 days, Pi drifts in a lifeboat with the tiger. Please understand: It's not a cute

Disney story about a boy and his kitten. It's an engaging, dangerous, and fascinating story about faith and survival.

As Pi adjusts to his grief and his terrifying situation—terror outside the boat, terror inside the boat—he plots to rid himself of the tiger. But in time, Pi discovers that the presence of the tiger gives him the courage and determination he needs to survive his ordeal.

It's quite a metaphor—that we may need to live with what we fear, what we do not understand, what challenges us—in order to survive a greater trial. As strange as it may seem, faith and fear are partners in the boat together. If we want to live our lives most fully and be present in each moment, we have to acknowledge and face our greatest fears.

What's fascinating about Martel's story is that Pi—the teenager—moved from plotting to rid himself of the tiger to understanding that the tiger was the key to his survival. We, too, may sometimes feel like a kid in a lifeboat with a tiger in the prow, hungry and thinking about his next meal. But as Pi came to realize, the adversities that come into our lives may, in fact, be critical to our survival.

What tiger is in your lifeboat? What challenges do you face?

What we learn from the book is that often we cannot shoot it, tranquilize it, train it to do tricks, or make it jump through hoops. Instead, we have to learn to live with it and learn from it; our fear of death not only should not be ignored, but it should be welcomed. If you think about it, this is also the lesson of Yom Kippur. On the holiest of days, we behave as if we are dead. We do not eat or drink. We do not make love. Traditional Jews wear white shrouds, as if they were dead. The point of these practices is not to create a Jewish version of Halloween. The point is to invite our fear of death into our lives because it is the only healthy way to deal with that fear.

Lessons of Our Greatest Fears

What happens when we invite death into our lives? What do we learn about ourselves? How can it make our lives more meaningful? I think we learn three important things.

First, we learn that death is not always the enemy. In the movie *Open Range,* Kevin Costner's character says that there are worse things than dying. When we or someone we love falls seriously ill and needs acute treatment, we should remember this observation. We often encourage such patients to submit to drastic and usually futile interventions that prolong suffering and make the final weeks of life intolerable.

Consider the story of the three sailors who are shipwrecked on a remote island and captured by a primitive tribe. They are tied up by the tribesmen and brought before a tribunal of elders. The elders give the first sailor a choice: "What would you rather have—death or Chi-Chi?" The sailor hesitates only a moment. "I know what death is, and I surely don't want it. I will take Chi-Chi." The sailor is then slowly skinned alive by the tribesmen and has his heart cut out while he is still conscious, after which he dies.

After watching this horrible ritual, the second sailor is brought before the tribunal. He is much more circumspect and thinks very carefully before giving his answer. "I certainly don't want to die, but I also don't want to be tortured and die anyway. But maybe Chi-Chi changes. Maybe it's a relative phenomenon. Maybe it won't happen to me. Given these limited choices, I guess I will take Chi-Chi." The second sailor is then subjected to the same ordeal, skinned alive, after which his heart is cut out while it is still beating.

The third sailor is then offered the same choice. His perspective is radically altered by the disturbing ritual he has witnessed. "Maybe death isn't all that bad. I certainly don't want Chi-Chi. I guess I will take death." The elders look a bit surprised and then say, "Okay, but first Chi-Chi."[2]

Dr. Timothy Quill, the author of this parable, explains that the sailors are patients, the tribesmen are medical practitioners, and the elders represent the attending physicians, whose treatment decisions may unintentionally prolong and dehumanize the dying process. Of course, there are times when patients are snatched from the brink of death and restored to long and productive lives by severe and agonizing treatments. But before opting for Chi-Chi, we should be very clear what it means, what odds we are up against, and what kind of life we'll have after we survive.

Mahatma Gandhi once observed, "No one can escape death. Then why be afraid of it? In fact, death is a friend who brings deliverance from suffering." This is not always the case, of course, but let's be honest: Sometimes we are fighting the wrong fight and the wrong enemy. For example, Jewish history is filled with stories of people who chose death over dishonor. There is even a name for it: *Kiddush Hashem*— sanctifying the name of God. The point is that death is not always the enemy. Sometimes it is more like a friend.

This leads to the second lesson: Our awareness of death gives our lives far more meaning. Indeed, death can be a great teacher. Imagine what life would be like if we were immortal. For a while it would be great. But after a few hundred years? What kind of existence would that be? The fact that we die teaches us something. Of course, we don't all learn the same lesson.

In ancient Rome, a human skeleton would be exhibited at parties. Partygoers would proclaim, "Let us enjoy life while we may." The prophet Isaiah criticizes those with such an approach when he mocks them, "Let us eat and drink, for tomorrow we die" (22:13). A wiser approach is found in Jewish tradition, among others. The Psalmist said it simply and profoundly: "Teach us to number our days that we may obtain a heart of wisdom" (Psalm 90:12). Or listen to the pithy advice of former British prime minister Benjamin Disraeli: "Life is too short to be little."

In the 1960s, Israeli author S. Y. Agnon won the Nobel Prize for literature. When the news was announced, all his friends rushed to his home in Talpiyyot, near Jerusalem, to say *mazal tov*. Hundreds of reporters and photographers came, too. The room was filled to overflowing. One of the photographers said, "Please sit at your desk and pretend you are writing something, so we can pose a picture of you that way." Agnon sat at the desk and scribbled something on a tablet, as the photographers took dozens of pictures of him posed that way. When the people finally left, someone went and looked at the tablet. Agnon had written five words, words that come from the High Holy Day prayer book: Our origin is dust and dust is our end. *Adam yisodo me'afar, visofo le'afar.* At this triumphant moment in his life, these were the words Agnon chose to remember. Did this diminish his joy? I think not. I think it heightened his spiritual appreciation of the moment. That's what death can do for us. Not only is death not the enemy. Death can be our teacher, our friend.

This leads to the third and last point. Ultimately, what lasts is not our final words. What lasts is the legacy we leave behind. When we learn to live with death, we also remember to create a lasting legacy while we can. After we die, what gets remembered? Consider the following quiz, which comes in two parts:

Here is part 1:

(1) Name the last five people who won the Academy Award for best actor.

(2) Name the last five Heisman trophy winners.

(3) Name the last five winners of the Ms. America contest.

(4) Name ten people who have won the Pulitzer Prize.

(5) Name the most valuable player in either baseball league for the last ten years.

(6) Name ten people who have won the Nobel Prize in science.

How did you do? Probably not too well. Remember these were not second-raters. These were the best in their fields. But the applause died down and the awards tarnished. The achievements get forgotten. Here is part 2:

(1) Name the teachers who inspired you.

(2) Name the friend who helped you get through a difficult time.

(3) Name three people who taught you something worthwhile.

(4) Name the people who have made you feel special and worthwhile.

(5) Name three people whom you admire.

(6) Name three people with whom you enjoy spending time.

I'll bet you did much better on the second part of the quiz. What is the moral? The people who are remembered are the people for whom we care and who care for us. If you want to leave a legacy, then care about other people. That's what counts.

Here is a story William B. Silverman, my rabbi in Kansas City, used to tell:

There was a young man named David Levy whose sole ambition from an early age was to be immortalized in human history. How this man wanted his name to be known! When he was a youngster, David Levy carved his name on a tree in the woods and he thought, "Now everybody who goes by this tree will know David Levy." His family moved away, and years later when he came back and went to the tree, he discovered that it had been chopped down. His name was gone. He then decided to chisel his name into a rock perched on top of a cliff. When he came back again many years later, he discovered that the rain and elements had eroded the letters. His name could no longer be deciphered. In time, he became a successful businessman and he declared, "I will erect an imposing building and I will call it the David Levy Building." So he did, but some years later, a fire burned the structure to the ground. Discouraged and despairing of ever perpetuating his name, he began to share his means with worthy causes and needy people.

One day he went to the ward of a children's hospital and brought toys for the poor children. One little girl looked up with gratitude in her eyes and said, "Mr. Levy, I will never forget you." He smiled as he answered, "Thank you, dear. That is sweet of you to say, but I'm afraid that after a while, you will." "Oh, no," the child responded. "I will never forget you, because, you see, your name is written upon my heart."

Do you want to leave a legacy? Write your name upon the hearts of the people you love. Will it cheat death? No. But it will ensure immortality. And having death with us in the lifeboat serves as a reminder that the time to leave the legacy is now, for no one can tell us for sure that we will be alive tomorrow.

Fear Not Your Fears

I began this final chapter speaking of final words. Here is what I hope you remember: When we confront death, as we should, we need to learn to accept it, even as we fear it. We should leave it in the lifeboat. And when we have it with us in our lifeboat, it should teach us three important lessons:

Death is not the enemy. There are things worse than death.

Our awareness of our immortality is what gives our lives meaning.

Instead of worrying about death, we should be worrying about our legacy.

Let me end this chapter with this final story:

Many centuries ago, there lived a great teacher. Three demons came to haunt the man as he meditated alone in a cave. These creatures represented the inner demons and conflicts—the fears—that arise in daily life. According to the legend, as the demons entered the calm meditative space of the cave (or, the mystic's conscious experience), the man smiled and welcomed them, urging them to sit with him by the warm fire and to "take tea."

The demons barked, "Aren't you horrified by our arrival?" The man responded, "Oh, not at all. At moments like these I am reminded to have compassion and mercy for myself. When the demons of fear, doubt, loathing, and anger appear, I am most grateful to be on the path of conscious spiritual growth, for then I can welcome you and open my heart to you, instead of running away and hiding. So, please, come and sit. Take tea with me. You are always welcome to emerge from the darkness and sit with me by the light of the fire. For it is only here that we may take tea together."

As the story teaches us, our fears are alive within us. They are real, and no amount of logic can banish them. But if we invite them in to sit beside the fire of consciousness, we can learn to live with them.

I end this book with the final words of a beloved teacher of generations of Reform rabbis, the late Rabbi Jakob Petuchowski. According to his son, on his deathbed, Rabbi Petuchowski chose profound words found at the end of *Adon Olam*. They are the best final words I have ever heard, and they are a source of comfort to me still.

> *Beyado afkid ruchi, b'et ishan v'a-ira.*
> *Ve-im ruchi g'viati, Adonai li v'lo ira.*
> *Into Your hand I assign my soul,*
>
> When I fall asleep and when I wake.
> To You I entrust my body too;
> The Eternal is with me; I need not fear.

Acknowledgments

I am so grateful to many people for making this book possible. I attended the Jewish Leaders Institute at Northwestern University in 2009 and from there was introduced by its director, Dinah Jacobs, to the concept of "the essence of strategy is denial" and found myself intrigued with the idea that we gain more by what we relinquish. Many decades ago, Professor Alan Lichterman of the University of Kansas enabled me to see a Zen release philosophy in the work of J. D. Salinger, a notion also at the core of this book. Along the way I have been given support by Rabbi Lawrence A. Hoffman; Stuart M. Matlins, publisher and founder of Jewish Lights; and Emily Wichland, vice president of Editorial and Production and a wonderful editor at Jewish Lights. I am also most grateful to the members and staff (including my assistant, Daphne Parker) of Temple Judea in Coral Gables, Florida, for inspiring and helping me to write this book, as well as the Institute for Jewish Spirituality. Last, but certainly not least, I am grateful for my beloved wife, Melanie Cole Goldberg.

Notes

Introduction

1. Nachman of Bratzlav, *Likutey Moharan* (Number 64) (Jerusalem: Breslov Research Institute, 2011). Translated by Jonathan Slater, Institute for Jewish Spirituality.
2. Avivah Zornberg, *The Murmuring Deep* (New York: Schocken Books, 2009), 70ff.

1 Reconnect with the Holiness in Time

1. Uploaded from Homiletics Online, October 1, 2012.
2. August 20, 2007.
3. From a sermon by Pastor Tom Lacey, Congregational Church of Boca Raton, February 14, 2010; www.churchofboca.org (accessed December 10, 2012).
4. Abraham Joshua Heschel, *The Sabbath: Its Meaning for Modern Man* (New York: Farrar, Straus and Giroux, 1951), 10.
5. Ibid., 89.

2 Keep a Tab on Mission Drift

1. Here's the actual, full quote: "In the long run, men hit only what they aim at. Therefore, they had better aim at something high." Read more at www.brainyquote.com/quotes/quotes/h/henrydavid163028. html#SFpHUifaDboVP10U.99 (accessed November 7, 2012).
2. *Harvard Business Review,* July–August 2010, 111.
3. Ibid., 49.

3 Let Go of Resentment

1. Donald McCullough, *Say Please, Say Thank You: The Respect We Owe One Another* (New York: G. P. Putnam, 1998), 258.

2. Michael McCullough, "Getting Revenge and Forgiveness," *On Being,* American Public Media (May 24, 2012).

3. Stephanie Dowrick, *Forgiveness and Other Acts of Love* (New York: W. W. Norton, 1998), 291–292.

4. Ibid., 292.

4 Downsize!

1. Babylonian Talmud, *Mishna Avot* 2:7.

2. Bob Moorehead, *Words Aptly Spoken* (self-published, 1995).

3. All biblical citations are based on the 1999 Jewish Publication Society translation, modified for gender sensitivity.

4. Rabbi Moti Rieber and Betsy Teutsch, cited on Reconstructionist Movement of America website, www2.jrf.org (accessed November 7, 2012).

5. William Henry Channing (1810–1884); www.goodreads.com (accessed December 10, 2012).

5 Be Present—Really Present—in Love

1. Cited in Sidney Greenberg, *Likrat Shabbat* (Bridgeport: Media Judaica), 74.

6 Respond to the Right Questions

1. Kenneth Paul Kramer, *Martin Buber's Spirituality* (New York: Rowman & Littlefield, 2012), 4.

2. *Midrash Genesis Rabbah*, comment on Genesis 12:1.

3. Anna Quindlen, commencement speech at Villanova University, class of 2000, June 23, 2000.

4. Stephanie Dowrick, *Forgiveness and Other Acts of Love* (New York: W. W. Norton, 1998), 210.

5. www.investigatorsanywhere.com/poems2.asp (accessed November 8, 2012).

8 Stress Less to Do More

1. *"Tzimtzum*: A Mystic Model for Contemporary Leadership," *Religious Education* 69, no. 6 (November–December 1974): 320–323.

9 Stop Ignoring Your Mental Garbage

1. Rabbi Jeff Roth, *Jewish Meditation Practices for Everyday Life* (Woodstock, Vt: Jewish Lights, 2009).

10 Take a Leap of Action

1. Joseph Telushkin, *Jewish Humor* (New York: William Morrow, 1992), 97.
2. From "Sing Out," translated by Emanuel Goldsmith; wwwinwardoutward.org (accessed September 28, 2007).
3. The Harris Poll #59, October 15, 2003.
4. Abraham Joshua Heschel, *Moral Grandeur and Spiritual Audacity*, edited by Susannah Heschel (New York: Farrar, Straus, and Giroux, 1996), 378.

11 Ask Less of the Earth

1. Bryan Urstadt, "Imagine There's No Oil: Scenes from a Liberal Apocalypse," *Harper's* (August, 2006).
2. *Midrash Leviticus Rabbah* 4:6.

13 Don't Underestimate the Power of Small Kindnesses

1. Maimonides, *Mishneh Torah, Hilchot Teshuvah*, 6:3.
2. Rachel Naomi Remen, *Kitchen Table Wisdom* (New York: Riverhead Books, 2006), 42–43.
3. Ibid., 58–59.
4. Stephanie Dowrick, *Forgiveness and Other Acts of Love* (New York: Norton, 1997), 192–193.

14 See the Divinity in Others

1. Eric Greenberg, "Manners and Morals," *Jewish Week*, January 15, 1999; www.jewishweek.com (accessed December 10, 2012).
2. "Excuse Me, But … What Ever Happened to Manners?" *USA Today*, December, 16, 1996.
3. This has been attributed to the late George Carlin.
4. Stephen L. Carter, *Civility: Manners, Morals, and the Etiquette of Democracy* (New York: Basic Books, 1998).
5. Cited in Carter, *Civility*, 4.
6. *Mishneh Torah, Hilchot Dei-ot* 6:7.

15 Recognize There Are No Guarantees

1. David Gelernter, *Time*, September 22, 1997.
2. Robert Gerzon, *Finding Serenity in the Age of Anxiety* (New York: Bantam, 1998), 209–210.
3. *Midrash Deuteronomy Rabbah* 9.
4. www.ziegler.ajula.edu (accessed December 10, 2012).
5. Kent Keith, "The Silent Revolution: Dynamic Leadership in the Student Council" (pamphlet, 1968).

16 Let Go of Fear by Facing It First

1. Dennis Gersten, MD, http://www.imagerynet.com/atlantis/techniques/overpain2.htm.
2. Joseph Heller, *Good as Gold* (New York: Simon & Schuster, 1997), 386.
3. Hamilton Jordan, *No Such Thing as a Bad Day* (New York: Pocket Books, 2000), 240.

17 Abandon Revenge and Resentment

1. Laura Blumenfeld, *Revenge: A Story of Hope* (New York: Simon & Schuster, 2002), 363.
2. Jay Winik, *April 1865: The Month That Saved America* (New York: HarperCollins, 2001), 362–363.

19 Hold on Tightly, Let Go Lightly

1. Cited in Albert Schweitzer, *The Words of Albert Schweitzer*, edited by Norman Cousins (Boston: Newmarket Press, 1996).
2. Danica Kirk, "Culture Heals the Hearts, Minds in War-Torn Sarajevo," *Los Angeles Times,* July 23, 1994.

21 Write Your Name Upon the Hearts of Others

1. Natalie Goldberg, *Writing Down the Bones* (Boston: Shambhala, 1986), 167.
2. Timothy Quill, *Death and Dignity: Making Choices and Taking Chances* (New York: W. W. Norton, 1993), 58.

Suggestions for
Further Reading

Benstein, Jeremy. *The Way Into Judaism and the Environment*. Woodstock, Vt.: Jewish Lights, 2006.

Breitman, Pattie, and Connie Hatch. *How to Say No Without Feeling Guilty: And Say Yes to More Time, and What Matters Most to You.* New York: Broadway, 2001.

Collins, Jim, and Morten T. Hansen. *Great By Choice: Uncertainty, Chaos, and Luck—Why Some Thrive Despite Them All.* New York: HarperBusiness, 2011.

Cootsona, Greg. *Say Yes to No: Using the Power of No to Create the Best in Life, Work, and Love.* New York: Doubleday, 2009.

Gallagher, Winifred. *Rapt: Attention and the Focused Life.* New York: Penguin, 2009.

Gefen, Nan Fink. *Discovering Jewish Meditation: Instruction & Guidance for Learning an Ancient Spiritual Practice,* 2nd ed. Woodstock, Vt.: Jewish Lights, 2011.

Isaacson, Walter. *Steve Jobs.* New York: Simon & Schuster, 2011.

Kaplan, Aryeh. *Jewish Meditation.* New York: Schocken Books, 1985.

Kraemer, Harry M. Jansen Jr. *From Values to Action: The Four Principles of Values-Based Leadership.* San Francisco: Jossey-Bass, 2011.

Roth, Jeff. *Jewish Meditation Practices for Everyday Life: Awakening Your Heart, Connecting with God.* Woodstock, Vt.: Jewish Lights, 2009.

Wareham, Beth. *The Power of No: How to Keep Blowhards and Bozos at Bay.* New York: Macmillan, 2009.

Bible Study / Midrash

The Book of Job: Annotated & Explained
Translation and Annotation by Donald Kraus; Foreword by Dr. Marc Brettler
Clarifies for today's readers what Job is, how to overcome difficulties in the text, and what it may mean for us. Features fresh translation and probing commentary.
5½ x 8½, 256 pp, Quality PB, 978-1-59473-389-5 **$16.99**

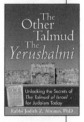

Masking and Unmasking Ourselves: Interpreting Biblical Texts on
Clothing & Identity *By Dr. Norman J. Cohen*
Presents ten Bible stories that involve clothing in an essential way, as a means of learning about the text, its characters and their interactions.
6 x 9, 240 pp, HC, 978-1-58023-461-0 **$24.99**

The Other Talmud—The Yerushalmi: Unlocking the Secrets of The
Talmud of Israel for Judaism Today *By Rabbi Judith Z. Abrams, PhD*
A fascinating—and stimulating—look at "the other Talmud" and the possibilities for Jewish life reflected there. 6 x 9, 256 pp, HC, 978-1-58023-463-4 **$24.99**

The Torah Revolution: Fourteen Truths That Changed the World
By Rabbi Reuven Hammer, PhD A unique look at the Torah and the revolutionary teachings of Moses embedded within it that gave birth to Judaism and influenced the world. 6 x 9, 240 pp, HC, 978-1-58023-457-3 **$24.99**

Ecclesiastes: Annotated & Explained
Translation and Annotation by Rabbi Rami Shapiro; Foreword by Rev. Barbara Cawthorne Crafton
5½ x 8½, 160 pp, Quality PB, 978-1-59473-287-4 **$16.99**

Ethics of the Sages: *Pirke Avot*—Annotated & Explained *Translation and Annotation by Rabbi Rami Shapiro* 5½ x 8½, 192 pp, Quality PB, 978-1-59473-207-2 **$16.99**

The Genesis of Leadership: What the Bible Teaches Us about Vision, Values and
Leading Change *By Rabbi Nathan Laufer; Foreword by Senator Joseph I. Lieberman*
6 x 9, 288 pp, Quality PB, 978-1-58023-352-1 **$18.99**

Hineini in Our Lives: Learning How to Respond to Others through 14 Biblical Texts and
Personal Stories *By Rabbi Norman J. Cohen, PhD* 6 x 9, 240 pp, Quality PB, 978-1-58023-274-6 **$16.99**

A Man's Responsibility: A Jewish Guide to Being a Son, a Partner in Marriage, a Father and a
Community Leader *By Rabbi Joseph B. Meszler* 6 x 9, 192 pp, Quality PB, 978-1-58023-435-1 **$16.99**

The Modern Men's Torah Commentary: New Insights from Jewish Men on the
54 Weekly Torah Portions *Edited by Rabbi Jeffrey K. Salkin*
6 x 9, 368 pp, HC, 978-1-58023-395-8 **$24.99**

Moses and the Journey to Leadership: Timeless Lessons of Effective Management
from the Bible and Today's Leaders *By Rabbi Norman J. Cohen, PhD*
6 x 9, 240 pp, Quality PB, 978-1-58023-351-4 **$18.99**; HC, 978-1-58023-227-2 **$21.99**

Proverbs: Annotated & Explained
Translation and Annotation by Rabbi Rami Shapiro
5½ x 8½, 288 pp, Quality PB, 978-1-59473-310-9 **$16.99**

Righteous Gentiles in the Hebrew Bible: Ancient Role Models for Sacred Relationships
By Rabbi Jeffrey K. Salkin; Foreword by Rabbi Harold M. Schulweis;
Preface by Phyllis Tickle 6 x 9, 192 pp, Quality PB, 978-1-58023-364-4 **$18.99**

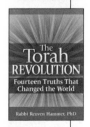

Sage Tales: Wisdom and Wonder from the Rabbis of the Talmud
By Rabbi Burton L. Visotzky 6 x 9, 256 pp, HC, 978-1-58023-456-6 **$24.99**

The Wisdom of Judaism: An Introduction to the Values of the Talmud
By Rabbi Dov Peretz Elkins 6 x 9, 192 pp, Quality PB, 978-1-58023-327-9 **$16.99**

Or phone, fax, mail or e-mail to: **JEWISH LIGHTS Publishing**
Sunset Farm Offices, Route 4 • P.O. Box 237 • Woodstock, Vermont 05091
Tel: (802) 457-4000 • Fax: (802) 457-4004 • www.jewishlights.com
Credit card orders: **(800) 962-4544** (8:30AM–5:30PM EST Monday–Friday)
Generous discounts on quantity orders. SATISFACTION GUARANTEED. Prices subject to change.

Ecology / Environment

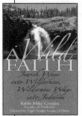

A Wild Faith: Jewish Ways into Wilderness, Wilderness Ways into Judaism
By Rabbi Mike Comins; Foreword by Nigel Savage 6 x 9, 240 pp, Quality PB, 978-1-58023-316-3 **$16.99**

Ecology & the Jewish Spirit: Where Nature & the Sacred Meet
Edited by Ellen Bernstein 6 x 9, 288 pp, Quality PB, 978-1-58023-082-7 **$18.99**

Torah of the Earth: Exploring 4,000 Years of Ecology in Jewish Thought
Vol. 1: Biblical Israel & Rabbinic Judaism; Vol. 2: Zionism & Eco-Judaism
Edited by Rabbi Arthur Waskow Vol. 1: 6 x 9, 272 pp, Quality PB, 978-1-58023-086-5 **$19.95**
Vol. 2: 6 x 9, 336 pp, Quality PB, 978-1-58023-087-2 **$19.95**

The Way Into Judaism and the Environment *By Jeremy Benstein, PhD*
6 x 9, 288 pp, Quality PB, 978-1-58023-368-2 **$18.99**; HC, 978-1-58023-268-5 **$24.99**

Graphic Novels / Graphic History

The Adventures of Rabbi Harvey: A Graphic Novel of Jewish Wisdom and Wit in the
Wild West *By Steve Sheinkin* 6 x 9, 144 pp, Full-color illus., Quality PB, 978-1-58023-310-1 **$16.99**

Rabbi Harvey Rides Again: A Graphic Novel of Jewish Folktales Let Loose in the
Wild West *By Steve Sheinkin* 6 x 9, 144 pp, Full-color illus., Quality PB, 978-1-58023-347-7 **$16.99**

Rabbi Harvey vs. the Wisdom Kid: A Graphic Novel of Dueling
Jewish Folktales in the Wild West *By Steve Sheinkin*
Rabbi Harvey's first book-length adventure—and toughest challenge.
6 x 9, 144 pp, Full-color illus., Quality PB, 978-1-58023-422-1 **$16.99**

The Story of the Jews: A 4,000-Year Adventure—A Graphic History Book
By Stan Mack 6 x 9, 288 pp, Illus., Quality PB, 978-1-58023-155-8 **$16.99**

Grief / Healing

Facing Illness, Finding God: How Judaism Can Help You and
Caregivers Cope When Body or Spirit Fails *By Rabbi Joseph B. Meszler*
Will help you find spiritual strength for healing amid the fear, pain and chaos of
illness. 6 x 9, 208 pp, Quality PB, 978-1-58023-423-8 **$16.99**

Midrash & Medicine: Healing Body and Soul in the Jewish Interpretive
Tradition *Edited by Rabbi William Cutter, PhD; Foreword by Michele F. Prince, LCSW, MAJCS*
Explores how midrash can help you see beyond the physical aspects of healing to
tune in to your spiritual source.
6 x 9, 352 pp, Quality PB, 978-1-58023-484-9 **$21.99**

Healing from Despair: Choosing Wholeness in a Broken World
By Rabbi Elie Kaplan Spitz with Erica Shapiro Taylor; Foreword by Abraham J. Twerski, MD
5½ x 8½, 208 pp, Quality PB, 978-1-58023-436-8 **$16.99**

Healing and the Jewish Imagination: Spiritual and Practical Perspectives on
Judaism and Health *Edited by Rabbi William Cutter, PhD*
6 x 9, 240 pp, Quality PB, 978-1-58023-373-6 **$19.99**

Grief in Our Seasons: A Mourner's Kaddish Companion *By Rabbi Kerry M. Olitzky*
4½ x 6½, 448 pp, Quality PB, 978-1-879045-55-2 **$15.95**

Healing of Soul, Healing of Body: Spiritual Leaders Unfold the Strength & Solace
in Psalms *Edited by Rabbi Simkha Y. Weintraub, LCSW*
6 x 9, 128 pp, 2-color illus. text, Quality PB, 978-1-879045-31-6 **$16.99**

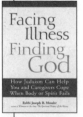

Mourning & Mitzvah, 2nd Edition: A Guided Journal for Walking the Mourner's
Path through Grief to Healing *By Rabbi Anne Brener, LCSW*
7½ x 9, 304 pp, Quality PB, 978-1-58023-113-8 **$19.99**

Tears of Sorrow, Seeds of Hope, 2nd Edition: A Jewish Spiritual Companion
for Infertility and Pregnancy Loss *By Rabbi Nina Beth Cardin*
6 x 9, 208 pp, Quality PB, 978-1-58023-233-3 **$18.99**

A Time to Mourn, a Time to Comfort, 2nd Edition: A Guide to Jewish
Bereavement *By Dr. Ron Wolfson; Foreword by Rabbi David J. Wolpe*
7 x 9, 384 pp, Quality PB, 978-1-58023-253-1 **$21.99**

When a Grandparent Dies: A Kid's Own Remembering Workbook for Dealing
with Shiva and the Year Beyond *By Nechama Liss-Levinson, PhD*
8 x 10, 48 pp, 2-color text, HC, 978-1-879045-44-6 **$15.95** *For ages 7–13*

Meditation

Jewish Meditation Practices for Everyday Life
Awakening Your Heart, Connecting with God
By Rabbi Jeff Roth
Offers a fresh take on meditation that draws on life experience and living life with greater clarity as opposed to the traditional method of rigorous study.
6 x 9, 224 pp, Quality PB, 978-1-58023-397-2 **$18.99**

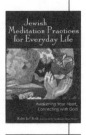

The Handbook of Jewish Meditation Practices
A Guide for Enriching the Sabbath and Other Days of Your Life
By Rabbi David A. Cooper Easy-to-learn meditation techniques.
6 x 9, 208 pp, Quality PB, 978-1-58023-102-2 **$16.95**

Discovering Jewish Meditation, 2nd Edition
Instruction & Guidance for Learning an Ancient Spiritual Practice
By Nan Fink Gefen, PhD 6 x 9, 208 pp, Quality PB, 978-1-58023-462-7 **$16.99**

Meditation from the Heart of Judaism
Today's Teachers Share Their Practices, Techniques, and Faith
Edited by Avram Davis 6 x 9, 256 pp, Quality PB, 978-1-58023-049-0 **$16.95**

Ritual / Sacred Practices

The Jewish Dream Book: The Key to Opening the Inner Meaning of
Your Dreams *By Vanessa L. Ochs, PhD, with Elizabeth Ochs; Illus. by Kristina Swarner*
Instructions for how modern people can perform ancient Jewish dream practices and dream interpretations drawn from the Jewish wisdom tradition.
8 x 8, 128 pp, Full-color illus., Deluxe PB w/ flaps, 978-1-58023-132-9 **$16.95**

God in Your Body: Kabbalah, Mindfulness and Embodied Spiritual Practice
By Jay Michaelson
The first comprehensive treatment of the body in Jewish spiritual practice and an essential guide to the sacred.
6 x 9, 272 pp, Quality PB, 978-1-58023-304-0 **$18.99**

The Book of Jewish Sacred Practices: CLAL's Guide to Everyday &
Holiday Rituals & Blessings *Edited by Rabbi Irwin Kula and Vanessa L. Ochs, PhD*
6 x 9, 368 pp, Quality PB, 978-1-58023-152-7 **$18.95**

Jewish Ritual: A Brief Introduction for Christians
By Rabbi Kerry M. Olitzky and Rabbi Daniel Judson
5½ x 8½, 144 pp, Quality PB, 978-1-58023-210-4 **$14.99**

The Rituals & Practices of a Jewish Life: A Handbook for Personal Spiritual
Renewal *Edited by Rabbi Kerry M. Olitzky and Rabbi Daniel Judson*
6 x 9, 272 pp, Illus., Quality PB, 978-1-58023-169-5 **$18.95**

The Sacred Art of Lovingkindness: Preparing to Practice
By Rabbi Rami Shapiro 5½ x 8½, 176 pp, Quality PB, 978-1-59473-151-8 **$16.99**
(A book from SkyLight Paths, Jewish Lights' sister imprint)

Science Fiction / Mystery & Detective Fiction

Criminal Kabbalah: An Intriguing Anthology of Jewish Mystery &
Detective Fiction *Edited by Lawrence W. Raphael; Foreword by Laurie R. King*
All-new stories from twelve of today's masters of mystery and detective fiction—sure to delight mystery buffs of all faith traditions.
6 x 9, 256 pp, Quality PB, 978-1-58023-109-1 **$16.95**

Mystery Midrash: An Anthology of Jewish Mystery & Detective Fiction
Edited by Lawrence W. Raphael; Preface by Joel Siegel
6 x 9, 304 pp, Quality PB, 978-1-58023-055-1 **$16.95**

Wandering Stars: An Anthology of Jewish Fantasy & Science Fiction
Edited by Jack Dann; Introduction by Isaac Asimov
6 x 9, 272 pp, Quality PB, 978-1-58023-005-6 **$18.99**

More Wandering Stars: An Anthology of Outstanding Stories of Jewish Fantasy and
Science Fiction *Edited by Jack Dann; Introduction by Isaac Asimov*
6 x 9, 192 pp, Quality PB, 978-1-58023-063-6 **$16.95**

Spirituality / Crafts

Jewish Threads: A Hands-On Guide to Stitching Spiritual Intention into Jewish Fabric Crafts *By Diana Drew with Robert Grayson*
Learn how to make your own Jewish fabric crafts with spiritual intention—a journey of creativity, imagination and inspiration. Thirty projects.
7 x 9, 288 pp, 8-page color insert, b/w illus., Quality PB Original, 978-1-58023-442-9 **$19.99**

(from SkyLight Paths, Jewish Lights' sister imprint)

Beading—The Creative Spirit: Finding Your Sacred Center through the Art of Beadwork *By Wendy Ellsworth*
Invites you on a spiritual pilgrimage into the kaleidoscope world of glass and color.
7 x 9, 240 pp, 8-page full-color insert, b/w photos and diagrams, Quality PB, 978-1-59473-267-6 **$18.99**

Contemplative Crochet: A Hands-On Guide for Interlocking Faith and Craft *By Cindy Crandall-Frazier; Foreword by Linda Skolnik*
Will take you on a path deeper into your crocheting and your spiritual awareness.
7 x 9, 208 pp, b/w photos, Quality PB, 978-1-59473-238-6 **$16.99**

The Knitting Way: A Guide to Spiritual Self-Discovery
By Linda Skolnik and Janice MacDaniels
Shows how to use knitting to strengthen your spiritual self.
7 x 9, 240 pp, b/w photos, Quality PB, 978-1-59473-079-5 **$16.99**

The Painting Path: Embodying Spiritual Discovery through Yoga, Brush and Color *By Linda Novick; Foreword by Richard Segalman*
Explores the divine connection you can experience through art.
7 x 9, 208 pp, 8-page full-color insert, b/w photos, Quality PB, 978-1-59473-226-3 **$18.99**

The Quilting Path: A Guide to Spiritual Self-Discovery through Fabric, Thread and Kabbalah *By Louise Silk* Explores how to cultivate personal growth through quilt making. 7 x 9, 192 pp, b/w photos, Quality PB, 978-1-59473-206-5 **$16.99**

The Scrapbooking Journey: A Hands-On Guide to Spiritual Discovery
By Cory Richardson-Lauve; Foreword by Stacy Julian
Reveals how this craft can become a practice used to deepen and shape your life.
7 x 9, 176 pp, 8-page full-color insert, b/w photos, Quality PB, 978-1-59473-216-4 **$18.99**

Travel

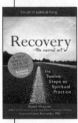

Israel—A Spiritual Travel Guide, 2nd Edition: A Companion for the Modern Jewish Pilgrim *By Rabbi Lawrence A. Hoffman, PhD*
Helps today's pilgrim tap into the deep spiritual meaning of the ancient—and modern—sites of the Holy Land.
4¾ x 10, 256 pp, Illus., Quality PB, 978-1-58023-261-6 **$18.99**
Also Available: **The Israel Mission Leader's Guide** 5½ x 8½, 16 pp, PB, 978-1-58023-085-8 **$4.95**

Twelve Steps

Recovery—The Sacred Art: The Twelve Steps as Spiritual Practice
By Rami Shapiro; Foreword by Joan Borysenko, PhD
Draws on insights and practices of different religious traditions to help you move more deeply into the universal spirituality of the Twelve Step system.
5½ x 8½, 240 pp, Quality PB Original, 978-1-59473-259-1 **$16.99**
(A book from SkyLight Paths, Jewish Lights' sister imprint)

100 Blessings Every Day: Daily Twelve Step Recovery Affirmations, Exercises for Personal Growth & Renewal Reflecting Seasons of the Jewish Year *By Rabbi Kerry M. Olitzky; Foreword by Rabbi Neil Gillman, PhD* 4½ x 6½, 432 pp, Quality PB, 978-1-879045-30-9 **$16.99**

Recovery from Codependence: A Jewish Twelve Steps Guide to Healing Your Soul
By Rabbi Kerry M. Olitzky 6 x 9, 160 pp, Quality PB, 978-1-879045-32-3 **$13.95**

Twelve Jewish Steps to Recovery, 2nd Edition: A Personal Guide to Turning from Alcoholism & Other Addictions—Drugs, Food, Gambling, Sex...
By Rabbi Kerry M. Olitzky and Stuart A. Copans, MD; Preface by Abraham J. Twerski, MD
6 x 9, 160 pp, Quality PB, 978-1-58023-409-2 **$16.99**

Social Justice

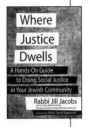

Where Justice Dwells
A Hands-On Guide to Doing Social Justice in Your Jewish Community
By Rabbi Jill Jacobs; Foreword by Rabbi David Saperstein
Provides ways to envision and act on your own ideals of social justice.
7 x 9, 288 pp, Quality PB Original, 978-1-58023-453-5 **$24.99**

There Shall Be No Needy
Pursuing Social Justice through Jewish Law and Tradition
By Rabbi Jill Jacobs; Foreword by Rabbi Elliot N. Dorff, PhD; Preface by Simon Greer
Confronts the most pressing issues of twenty-first-century America from a deeply
Jewish perspective. 6 x 9, 288 pp, Quality PB, 978-1-58023-425-2 **$16.99**
There Shall Be No Needy Teacher's Guide 8½ x 11, 56 pp, PB, 978-1-58023-429-0 **$8.99**

Conscience
The Duty to Obey and the Duty to Disobey
By Rabbi Harold M. Schulweis
Examines the idea of conscience and the role conscience plays in our relationships
to government, law, ethics, religion, human nature, God—and to each other.
6 x 9, 160 pp, Quality PB, 978-1-58023-419-1 **$16.99**; HC, 978-1-58023-375-0 **$19.99**

Judaism and Justice
The Jewish Passion to Repair the World
By Rabbi Sidney Schwarz; Foreword by Ruth Messinger
Explores the relationship between Judaism, social justice and the Jewish identity
of American Jews. 6 x 9, 352 pp, Quality PB, 978-1-58023-353-8 **$19.99**

Spirituality / Women's Interest

New Jewish Feminism
Probing the Past, Forging the Future
Edited by Rabbi Elyse Goldstein; Foreword by Anita Diamant
Looks at the growth and accomplishments of Jewish feminism and what they
mean for Jewish women today and tomorrow.
6 x 9, 480 pp, HC, 978-1-58023-359-0 **$24.99**

The Divine Feminine in Biblical Wisdom Literature
Selections Annotated & Explained
Translation & Annotation by Rabbi Rami Shapiro
5½ x 8½, 240 pp, Quality PB, 978-1-59473-109-9 **$16.99**
(A book from SkyLight Paths, Jewish Lights' sister imprint)

The Quotable Jewish Woman
Wisdom, Inspiration & Humor from the Mind & Heart
Edited by Elaine Bernstein Partnow
6 x 9, 496 pp, Quality PB, 978-1-58023-236-4 **$19.99**

The Women's Haftarah Commentary
New Insights from Women Rabbis on the 54 Weekly Haftarah Portions,
the 5 Megillot & Special Shabbatot
Edited by Rabbi Elyse Goldstein
Illuminates the historical significance of female portrayals in the Haftarah and the
Five Megillot. 6 x 9, 560 pp, Quality PB, 978-1-58023-371-2 **$19.99**

The Women's Torah Commentary
New Insights from Women Rabbis on the 54 Weekly Torah Portions
Edited by Rabbi Elyse Goldstein
Over fifty women rabbis offer inspiring insights on the Torah, in a week-by-week format.
6 x 9, 496 pp, Quality PB, 978-1-58023-370-5 **$19.99**; HC, 978-1-58023-076-6 **$34.95**

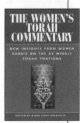

Inspiration

God of Me: Imagining God throughout Your Lifetime
By Rabbi David Lyon Helps you cut through preconceived ideas of God and dogmas that stifle your creativity when thinking about your personal relationship with God. 6 x 9, 176 pp, Quality PB, 978-1-58023-452-8 **$16.99**

The God Upgrade: Finding Your 21st-Century Spirituality in Judaism's 5,000-Year-Old Tradition *By Rabbi Jamie Korngold; Foreword by Rabbi Harold M. Schulweis* A provocative look at how our changing God concepts have shaped every aspect of Judaism. 6 x 9, 176 pp, Quality PB, 978-1-58023-443-6 **$15.99**

The Seven Questions You're Asked in Heaven: Reviewing and Renewing Your Life on Earth *By Dr. Ron Wolfson* An intriguing and entertaining resource for living a life that matters. 6 x 9, 176 pp, Quality PB, 978-1-58023-407-8 **$16.99**

Happiness and the Human Spirit: The Spirituality of Becoming the Best You Can Be *By Rabbi Abraham J. Twerski, MD*
Shows you that true happiness is attainable once you stop looking outside yourself for the source. 6 x 9, 176 pp, Quality PB, 978-1-58023-404-7 **$16.99**; HC, 978-1-58023-343-9 **$19.99**

A Formula for Proper Living: Practical Lessons from Life and Torah
By Rabbi Abraham J. Twerski, MD 6 x 9, 144 pp, HC, 978-1-58023-402-3 **$19.99**

The Bridge to Forgiveness: Stories and Prayers for Finding God and Restoring Wholeness *By Rabbi Karyn D. Kedar* 6 x 9, 176 pp, Quality PB, 978-1-58023-451-1 **$16.99**

The Empty Chair: Finding Hope and Joy—Timeless Wisdom from a Hasidic Master, Rebbe Nachman of Breslov *Adapted by Moshe Mykoff and the Breslov Research Institute* 4 x 6, 128 pp, Deluxe PB w/ flaps, 978-1-879045-67-5 **$9.99**

The Gentle Weapon: Prayers for Everyday and Not-So-Everyday Moments— Timeless Wisdom from the Teachings of the Hasidic Master, Rebbe Nachman of Breslov *Adapted by Moshe Mykoff and S. C. Mizrahi, together with the Breslov Research Institute* 4 x 6, 144 pp, Deluxe PB w/ flaps, 978-1-58023-022-3 **$9.99**

God Whispers: Stories of the Soul, Lessons of the Heart *By Rabbi Karyn D. Kedar* 6 x 9, 176 pp, Quality PB, 978-1-58023-088-9 **$15.95**

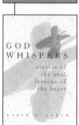

God's To-Do List: 103 Ways to Be an Angel and Do God's Work on Earth
By Dr. Ron Wolfson 6 x 9, 144 pp, Quality PB, 978-1-58023-301-9 **$16.99**

Jewish Stories from Heaven and Earth: Inspiring Tales to Nourish the Heart and Soul *Edited by Rabbi Dov Peretz Elkins* 6 x 9, 304 pp, Quality PB, 978-1-58023-363-7 **$16.99**

Life's Daily Blessings: Inspiring Reflections on Gratitude and Joy for Every Day, Based on Jewish Wisdom *By Rabbi Kerry M. Olitzky* 4½ x 6½, 368 pp, Quality PB, 978-1-58023-396-5 **$16.99**

Restful Reflections: Nighttime Inspiration to Calm the Soul, Based on Jewish Wisdom *By Rabbi Kerry M. Olitzky and Rabbi Lori Forman-Jacobi* 5 x 8, 352 pp, Quality PB, 978-1-58023-091-9 **$16.99**

Sacred Intentions: Morning Inspiration to Strengthen the Spirit, Based on Jewish Wisdom *By Rabbi Kerry M. Olitzky and Rabbi Lori Forman-Jacobi* 4½ x 6½, 448 pp, Quality PB, 978-1-58023-061-2 **$16.99**

Kabbalah / Mysticism

Jewish Mysticism and the Spiritual Life: Classical Texts, Contemporary Reflections *Edited by Dr. Lawrence Fine, Dr. Eitan Fishbane and Rabbi Or N. Rose* Inspirational and thought-provoking materials for contemplation, discussion and action. 6 x 9, 256 pp, HC, 978-1-58023-434-4 **$24.99**

Ehyeh: A Kabbalah for Tomorrow
By Rabbi Arthur Green, PhD 6 x 9, 224 pp, Quality PB, 978-1-58023-213-5 **$18.99**

The Gift of Kabbalah: Discovering the Secrets of Heaven, Renewing Your Life on Earth *By Tamar Frankiel, PhD* 6 x 9, 256 pp, Quality PB, 978-1-58023-141-1 **$16.95**

Seek My Face: A Jewish Mystical Theology *By Rabbi Arthur Green, PhD* 6 x 9, 304 pp, Quality PB, 978-1-58023-130-5 **$19.95**

Zohar: Annotated & Explained *Translation & Annotation by Dr. Daniel C. Matt; Foreword by Andrew Harvey* 5½ x 8½, 176 pp, Quality PB, 978-1-893361-51-5 **$16.99** *(A book from SkyLight Paths, Jewish Lights' sister imprint)*

Spirituality

The Jewish Lights Spirituality Handbook: A Guide to Understanding, Exploring & Living a Spiritual Life *Edited by Stuart M. Matlins*
What exactly is "Jewish" about spirituality? How do I make it a part of my life? Fifty of today's foremost spiritual leaders share their ideas and experience with us.
6 x 9, 456 pp, Quality PB, 978-1-58023-093-3 **$19.99**

The Sabbath Soul: Mystical Reflections on the Transformative Power of Holy Time *Selection, Translation and Commentary by Eitan Fishbane, PhD*
Explores the writings of mystical masters of Hasidism. Provides translations and interpretations of a wide range of Hasidic sources previously unavailable in English that reflect the spiritual transformation that takes place on the seventh day.
6 x 9, 208 pp, Quality PB, 978-1-58023-459-7 **$18.99**

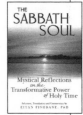

Repentance: The Meaning and Practice of *Teshuvah*
By Dr. Louis E. Newman; Foreword by Rabbi Harold M. Schulweis; Preface by Rabbi Karyn D. Kedar
Examines both the practical and philosophical dimensions of *teshuvah*, Judaism's core religious-moral teaching on repentance, and its value for us—Jews and non-Jews alike—today. 6 x 9, 256 pp, HC, 978-1-58023-426-9 **$24.99**

Aleph-Bet Yoga: Embodying the Hebrew Letters for Physical and Spiritual Well-Being
By Steven A. Rapp; Foreword by Tamar Frankiel, PhD, and Judy Greenfeld; Preface by Hart Lazer
7 x 10, 128 pp, b/w photos, Quality PB, Lay-flat binding, 978-1-58023-162-6 **$16.95**

A Book of Life: Embracing Judaism as a Spiritual Practice
By Rabbi Michael Strassfeld 6 x 9, 544 pp, Quality PB, 978-1-58023-247-0 **$19.99**

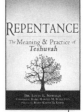

Bringing the Psalms to Life: How to Understand and Use the Book of Psalms
By Rabbi Daniel F. Polish, PhD 6 x 9, 208 pp, Quality PB, 978-1-58023-157-2 **$16.95**

Does the Soul Survive? A Jewish Journey to Belief in Afterlife, Past Lives & Living with Purpose *By Rabbi Elie Kaplan Spitz; Foreword by Brian L. Weiss, MD*
6 x 9, 288 pp, Quality PB, 978-1-58023-165-7 **$16.99**

Entering the Temple of Dreams: Jewish Prayers, Movements and Meditations for the End of the Day *By Tamar Frankiel, PhD, and Judy Greenfeld*
7 x 10, 192 pp, illus., Quality PB, 978-1-58023-079-7 **$16.95**

First Steps to a New Jewish Spirit: Reb Zalman's Guide to Recapturing the Intimacy & Ecstasy in Your Relationship with God *By Rabbi Zalman M. Schachter-Shalomi with Donald Gropman* 6 x 9, 144 pp, Quality PB, 978-1-58023-182-4 **$16.95**

Foundations of Sephardic Spirituality: The Inner Life of Jews of the Ottoman Empire
By Rabbi Marc D. Angel, PhD 6 x 9, 224 pp, Quality PB, 978-1-58023-341-5 **$18.99**

God & the Big Bang: Discovering Harmony between Science & Spirituality
By Dr. Daniel C. Matt 6 x 9, 216 pp, Quality PB, 978-1-879045-89-7 **$18.99**

God in Our Relationships: Spirituality between People from the Teachings of Martin Buber *By Rabbi Dennis S. Ross* 5½ x 8½, 160 pp, Quality PB, 978-1-58023-147-3 **$16.95**

Judaism, Physics and God: Searching for Sacred Metaphors in a Post-Einstein World
By Rabbi David W. Nelson 6 x 9, 352 pp, Quality PB, inc. reader's discussion guide,
978-1-58023-306-4 **$18.99**; HC, 352 pp, 978-1-58023-252-4 **$24.99**

Meaning & Mitzvah: Daily Practices for Reclaiming Judaism through Prayer, God, Torah, Hebrew, Mitzvot and Peoplehood *By Rabbi Goldie Milgram*
7 x 9, 336 pp, Quality PB, 978-1-58023-256-2 **$19.99**

Minding the Temple of the Soul: Balancing Body, Mind, and Spirit through Traditional Jewish Prayer, Movement, and Meditation *By Tamar Frankiel, PhD, and Judy Greenfeld*
7 x 10, 184 pp, Illus., Quality PB, 978-1-879045-64-4 **$18.99**

One God Clapping: The Spiritual Path of a Zen Rabbi *By Rabbi Alan Lew with Sherril Jaffe*
5¼ x 8¼, 336 pp, Quality PB, 978-1-58023-115-2 **$16.95**

The Soul of the Story: Meetings with Remarkable People
By Rabbi David Zeller 6 x 9, 288 pp, HC, 978-1-58023-272-2 **$21.99**

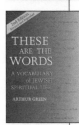

Tanya, the Masterpiece of Hasidic Wisdom: Selections Annotated & Explained
Translation & Annotation by Rabbi Rami Shapiro; Foreword by Rabbi Zalman M. Schachter-Shalomi
5½ x 8½, 240 pp, Quality PB, 978-1-59473-275-1 **$16.99**

These Are the Words, 2nd Edition: A Vocabulary of Jewish Spiritual Life
By Rabbi Arthur Green, PhD 6 x 9, 320 pp, Quality PB, 978-1-58023-494-8 **$19.99**

About Jewish Lights

People of all faiths and backgrounds yearn for books that attract, engage, educate, and spiritually inspire.

Our principal goal is to stimulate thought and help all people learn about who the Jewish People are, where they come from, and what the future can be made to hold. While people of our diverse Jewish heritage are the primary audience, our books speak to people in the Christian world as well and will broaden their understanding of Judaism and the roots of their own faith.

We bring to you authors who are at the forefront of spiritual thought and experience. While each has something different to say, they all say it in a voice that you can hear.

Our books are designed to welcome you and then to engage, stimulate, and inspire. We judge our success not only by whether or not our books are beautiful and commercially successful, but by whether or not they make a difference in your life.

For your information and convenience, at the back of this book we have provided a list of other Jewish Lights books you might find interesting and useful. They cover all the categories of your life:

Bar/Bat Mitzvah
Bible Study / Midrash
Children's Books
Congregation Resources
Current Events / History
Ecology / Environment
Fiction: Mystery, Science Fiction
Grief / Healing
Holidays / Holy Days
Inspiration
Kabbalah / Mysticism / Enneagram

Life Cycle
Meditation
Men's Interest
Parenting
Prayer / Ritual / Sacred Practice
Social Justice
Spirituality
Theology / Philosophy
Travel
Twelve Steps
Women's Interest

Stuart M. Matlins, Publisher

Or phone, fax, mail or e-mail to: **JEWISH LIGHTS Publishing**
Sunset Farm Offices, Route 4 • P.O. Box 237 • Woodstock, Vermont 05091
Tel: (802) 457-4000 • Fax: (802) 457-4004 • www.jewishlights.com
Credit card orders: (800) 962-4544 (8:30AM–5:30PM EST Monday–Friday)
Generous discounts on quantity orders. SATISFACTION GUARANTEED. Prices subject to change.

For more information about each book, visit our website at www.jewishlights.com